hamlyn
Quick**Cook**

hamlyn
QuickCook
Pasta

Recipes by Emma Lewis

Every dish, three ways—you choose!
30 minutes | 20 minutes | 10 minutes

An Hachette UK company
www.hachette.co.uk

First published in Great Britain in 2012 by Hamlyn,
a division of Octopus Publishing Group Ltd
Endeavour House, 189 Shaftesbury Avenue, London WC2H 8JY
www.octopusbooks.co.uk

Distributed in the US by Hachette Book Group USA
237 Park Avenue, New York, NY 10017 USA
www.octopusbooksusa.com

Distributed in Canada by Canadian Manda Group
165 Dufferin Street, Toronto, Ontario, Canada M6K 3H6

Recipes by Emma Lewis
Copyright © Octopus Publishing Group Ltd 2012

ISBN: 978-060062-400-4

Printed and bound in China

1 2 3 4 5 6 7 8 9 10

Standard level spoon measurements are used in all recipes

Ovens should be preheated to the specified temperature. If using a fan-assisted
oven, follow the manufacturer's instructions for adjusting the time and temperature.

Eggs should be medium unless otherwise stated. The FDA advises that eggs should
not be consumed raw. This book contains some dishes made with raw or lightly
cooked eggs. It is prudent for more vulnerable people, such as pregnant and nursing
mothers, invalids, the elderly, babies, and young children, to avoid uncooked or lightly
cooked dishes made with eggs.

This book includes dishes made with nuts and nut derivatives. It is advisable for those
with known allergic reactions to nuts and nut derivatives and those who may be
potentially vulnerable to these allergies, such as pregnant and nursing mothers,
invalids, the elderly, babies, and children, to avoid dishes made with nuts and nut oils.
It is also prudent to check the labels of prepared ingredients for the possible inclusion
of nut derivatives.

Executive Editor: **Eleanor Maxfield**
Editor: **Joanne Wilson**
Copy-Editor: **Jo Murray**
Art Director: **Jonathan Christie**
Design: **www.gradedesign.com**
Art Direction: **Juliette Norsworthy & Tracy Killick**
Photographer: **Craig Robertson**
Home Economist: **Emma Lewis**
Stylist: **Isabel De Cordova**
Production: **David Hearne**

Contents

Introduction

30 20 10—Quick, Quicker, Quickest

This book offers a new and flexible approach to meal-planning for busy cooks, letting you choose the recipe option that best fits the time you have available. Inside you will find 360 dishes that will inspire and motivate you to get cooking every day of the year. All the recipes take a maximum of 30 minutes to cook. Some take as little as 20 minutes and, amazingly, many take only 10 minutes. With a bit of preparation, you can easily try out one new recipe from this book each night and slowly you will be able to build a wide and exciting portfolio of recipes to suit your needs.

How Does it Work?

Every recipe in the QuickCook series can be cooked one of three ways—a 30-minute version, a 20-minute version, or a super-quick and easy 10-minute version. At the beginning of each chapter you'll find recipes listed by time. Choose a dish based on how much time you have and turn to that page.

You'll find the main recipe in the middle of the page accompanied by a beautiful photograph, as well as two time-variation recipes below.

If you enjoy the dish, you can go back and cook the other time options another time. If you liked the 20-minute Spaghetti Salsa Verde with Broiled Chicken, but only have 10 minutes to spare, then you'll find a way to cook it using cheat ingredients or clever shortcuts.

If you love the ingredients and flavors of the 10-minute Chorizo and Red Pepper Pasta, why not try something more substantial like the 20-minute Paella-style Red Pepper Pasta, or be inspired to cook a more elaborate version like a Pasta with Rich Red Pepper Sauce. Alternatively, browse through all of the 360 delicious recipes, find something that takes your eye—then cook the version that fits your time frame.

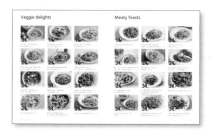

Or, for easy inspiration, turn to the gallery on pages 12–19 to get an instant overview by themes, such as Veggie Delights or Meaty Feasts.

QuickCook online

To make life even easier, you can use the special code on each recipe page to email yourself a recipe card for printing, or email a text-only shopping list to your phone. Go to www.hamlynquickcook.com and enter the recipe code at the bottom of each page.

PAS-MIDW-QEC

QuickCook Pasta

For many years the story was that Marco Polo invented pasta when he tasted noodles on his travels to China and spread the word as soon as he returned to Italy. It's a lovely image, but historians think Europeans have been enjoying pasta for many years, certainly since Roman times. No doubt it's maintained its popularity because it's good value, quick to cook, and can be enjoyed with so many different flavors. Even within Italy, you'll find plenty of variations. Northern Italy tends to favor rich sauces such as the famous ragu alla Bolognese or Genovese pesto, while the central zone favors simpler dishes like carbonara and amatriciana. In the South you'll find lighter sauces with plenty of olive oil, tomatoes, and often a scattering of vegetables and seafood. From its homeland in Italy, a love of pasta has spread around the world. From new classics such as alfredo sauce or penne a la vodka, developed in the USA to more exotic flavors found in Spanish or even Mexican inspired pasta dishes, to the classic child-friendly macaroni and cheese, you can find fast and satisfying dinners.

QuickCook Techniques and Tips

How to cook pasta

To start, you'll need your largest pan. Pasta needs a lot of water to cook in—at least 3 quarts for 14 oz. Otherwise it not only won't cook evenly, but it tends to turn gummy. You will also need plenty of salt—the water should taste a little of the sea. This means adding about 1 tablespoon of salt to the pan. This will seem like a lot, but remember most of it will be drained away, leaving the pasta delicately flavored. People often add some olive oil to the pan, but cooked properly, this isn't really necessary.

Make sure your water is brought to a very vigorous rolling boil over your highest heat setting. Add the pasta all in one go, so it cooks uniformly. Stir with a long spoon to help prevent sticking, then let it return to a boil. Allow to cook, stirring occasionally, and lowering the heat just a little if it threatens to boil over. Start timing from the moment the pan returns to a boil. The cooking time will depend on the type of pasta and the brand. Fresh pasta cooks in a matter of minutes, while some pastas made from high-quality hard wheat take 15 minutes.

How do you know it's done?

It's best to check the pasta about 2 minutes before the package instructions suggest. It should be al dente which means "to the tooth," soft and tender but with a little bite. You don't want overcooked mushy pasta which has lost all its chewy qualities. If it's underdone it will still have a chalky core and the slight taste of raw flour.

Draining

Have a colander to hand and when the pasta is ready, scoop out half a mugful of water (you might need this later on when adding the sauce), then drain straight away. Do not drain too thoroughly because the hot pasta keeps cooking, and the water will evaporate, and dry out the pasta. It should remain slippery so it can be mixed with the sauce.

The final mixing together

Some people serve pasta and sauce separately, but to fully appreciate the flavors you need to toss them together. Tip the pasta back into the cooking pan and pour over the sauce. You want enough sauce to moisten but not drown or overwhelm the pasta. You will probably also need to add a couple of tablespoons of cooking water to the pan. Have some warmed bowls to hand and then serve straight away— remember pasta waits for no one.

QuickCook Ingredients/Pantry

A well-stocked pantry is an asset to any kitchen, and is worth building up when you have time. The following ingredients are used in some of the recipes, especially the 10-minute variations, as sometimes "ready-cooked" (meaning store-bought) ingredients that can be bought for a reasonable price, are a sensible alternative to "homemade."

Jars of store-bought tomato pasta sauce that can be used as a base, or on their own, are occassionally listed. Buy the best you can afford, preferably from the chiller cabinet or go for organic, with no added flavorings. Store-bought roasted chicken breast fillets can be a reasonably priced alternative, and keep in the refrigerator for a few days. As for sauce additions, store-bought cooked and peeled chestnuts keep for a long time in the pantry and are surprisingly versatile. Store-bought ready-cooked caramelized onion, and easy-fried onion which comes in a jar also both save time.

Where store-bought red, green pesto and hummus are suggested, we mean the fresh pesto in containers, found in the deli section of your local supermarket. Experiment and you will find a supermarket-own brand that you like best. Sometimes we have suggested using packages of tortelloni or gnocchi as well as roasted red peppers from a jar, drained. Ready-cooked lentils in packs or cans, can speed up the cooking time, and avoids soaking overnight. Cans of tuna and sardines pack delicious tastes that are a good base for sauces.

Choosing the right pasta
Fresh or dry? People often spend more money on fresh pasta, but this isn't always the best option. Finding truly fresh pasta is a challenge, and making it is very time-consuming, so it can be better to choose a really good-quality dry option. Italian ones are generally the best, probably because pasta manufacturers in Italy have to adhere to a strict set of guidelines. Choose pasta made from one hundred percent durum wheat. This is a very hard type of wheat and means the pasta will maintain its shape, texture, and flavor well. It's using this type of flour which makes pasta different from other noodles as it's so malleable and can be twisted, stretched, and pressed to make hundreds of different shapes. In addition to plain pasta you can also find golden egg pasta. This is silkier and smoother and works best with rich butter and cream-based sauces which come from the North of Italy while plain pasta is better with oil sauces more traditional in the South. If you are lucky enough to live near a specialty Italian store which makes pasta in-house you can buy freshly rolled sheets of pasta. Unlike fresh lasagna sold pre-packaged in supermarkets, these will keep only for a day or two and are soft and malleable enough for you to make your own ravioli and tortelloni. They are a treat, cut into small strips, used in a lasagna. For the health conscious there is now a wide variety of pasta shapes made from whole wheat. This darker pasta is made from whole grain flour which is healthier than white, refined flour but often will take longer to cook. In health food stores and the specialty section of supermarkets you'll also see lots of popular pasta shapes which are gluten-free and can

be eaten by those with wheat allergy. These are normally made from rice and corn flours and can be used instead of the regular wheat varieties. If you're feeling adventurous you can also find pasta colored with vegetables and dyes—green spinach pasta, but purple beet is also good as are orange squash and deep black squid ink varieties.

Types of pasta

Just about every pasta shape that you could imagine exists, from novelty reindeer or tiny star-shaped pasta for soup to classics like spaghetti. As a rule you can divide pasta into three types—filled pastas such as tortelloni, or their smaller cousins tortellini, ravioli, and cannelloni tubes, long strands of pasta, and short tubes and pasta shapes. While a lot depends on your preference (and what pasta you have in the house), for the best results you should try to match your sauce to the pasta you are using. As a general rule short tubes of pasta and pasta shapes are better at trapping in the flavors of chunky sauces, long strands are better paired with thinner delicate sauces.

The best known of these is of course spaghetti, but thicker linguine and thicker still, flat, tagliatelle are also popular as are the very thin strands called angel hair or capellini. If you want to try something different, look out for bucatini, thick hollow strands, or pappardelle which are very broad ribbons.

Penne is an ever popular pasta tube along with the fatter rigatoni and kids' favorite macaroni. You can also use shell-shaped pasta such as conchiglie or very large tubes such as tubetti. Other dependable shapes include farfalle, the pretty butterfly style, and twists of fusilli. Artisan pastas are more popular like uneven thick trofie and the flat disks of orecchiette.

How much pasta

There is no firm rule on how much pasta to cook. In Italy pasta is normally served as part of a larger meal, while in other countries it's the main event. But a good rule of thumb is to allow about 4 oz of pasta per person for a main meal. The recipes in this book are easy to scale up or down for different numbers, and it's simple to add another handful to the pan if your diners look a little hungry. Also, if you wish to use a fresh pasta where dried is suggested, scale the quantity up for fresh. More fresh pasta (roughly one-third of the weight again) will be needed to make up the same finished amount.

Pasta bakes

Hearty and wholesome, these mouthwatering dishes make for the coziest of meals.

Spicy Mushroom Rigatoni Bake 52

Chicken, Bacon, and Asparagus Pasta Bake 86

Cheesy Tomato Pasta Bake 128

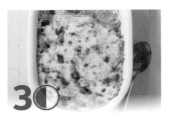

Ham and Zucchini Lasagne 142

Pasta Rolls with Red Pepper and Ricotta 146

Broccoli and Ham Pasta Bake 164

Tuna and Corn Pasta Bake 168

Spinach and Ricotta Cannelloni 172

Hearty Sausage and Spinach Pasta Bake 174

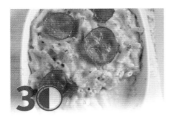

Sin-free Macaroni and Cheese with Tomato 226

Blue Cheese and Cauliflower Cannelloni 258

Macaroni Shrimp Gratin 266

Something a little bit different

Perfect for everyday eating, easy, unusual pasta dishes.

Individual Bacon Frittatas 32

Herby Fettucine with Fried Eggs 38

Creamy Chicken and Artichoke Frittata 62

Spanish Seafood Pasta 116

Farfalle with Chicken Corn Bites and Red Pepper Sauce 148

Seafood Spaghetti in a Creamy Sauce 150

Skillet Macaroni and Cheese 160

Open Butternut Squash and Ricotta Lasagna 188

Spiced Lentils with Angel Hair Pasta 202

Creamy Vodka and Tomato Taconelli 240

Salmon and Zucchini Pasta 242

Sweet Potato Pockets with Sage Butter and Amaretti 278

Soups and salads

Light and healthy appetizers, mains, and snacks.

Zucchini, Pea, and Pasta Soup with Pesto 24

Spicy Fish Soup 36

Greek Style Tomato, Olive, and Feta Pasta Salad 44

Salmon Pasta Salad with Dill Dressing 48

Fresh Herb Pasta Salad 50

Red Pepper Arugula and Parmesan Pasta salad 64

Classic Minestrone 132

No-chop Tomato and Arugula Pasta Salad 136

Tomato Soup with Pasta Shapes 140

Turkey Meatball and Pasta Soup 182

Pasta Nicoise 190

Light Clam and Tomato Broth 232

Spice up your spaghetti

The 10-minute staple is adaptable for all occasions.

Spaghettini with Tomato and Basil Butter 68

Spaghetti with Watercress Pesto and Blue Cheese 80

Creamy Anchovy, Lemon, and Arugula Spaghetti 88

Spaghetti Salsa Verde with Broiled Chicken 94

Spaghetti Carbonara 130

Easy Sausage Spaghetti Bolognese 158

Arugula, Chilli, and Ricotta Spaghetti 184

Spaghetti with Kale and Gruyère 192

Spaghetti with Mini Tuna Balls 206

Red Pepper and Walnut Spaghetti 214

Spaghetti with Angler Fish, Mussels and Fennel 248

Fiery Black Spaghetti with Squid 254

Fish and seafood

A medley of fresh fish dishes, for lunch, and suppers.

Tuna and White Bean Pasta with Gremolata 70

Linguine with Seafood in a Tomato Sauce 92

Lemony Conchiglie with Tuna and Capers 100

Bucatini with Sardines and Fennel 112

Salmon and Leek Conchiglie 166

Gnocchi with Salmon in a Chilli Tomato Sauce 218

Linguine with Tuna Sashimi and Arugula 234

Zingy Crab Angel Hair Pasta 236

Seared Seabass with Warm Pasta Salad and Basil Oil 252

Pasta with Salmon, Arugula and Red Onion 268

Creamy Lobster Fettuccine 270

Creamy Tomato Pasta with Shrimp 274

Cheesy treats

Cheese-led pasta meals that are full of flavour.

**Spaghetti with Beet
and Goats' Cheese** 26

**Penne with Broccoli and
Blue Cheese Sauce** 34

Herby Goat Cheese Pasta 46

**Eggplant and Mozzarella Fusilli
Lunghi** 82

**Creamy Gorgonzola
Gnocchi** 106

**Linguine with Endive,
Pancetta, and Mascarpone**
108

**Shrimp, Tomato, and
Feta Rigatoni** 110

**Sweet Potato and
Spinach Penne** 120

**Four-cheese Pasta
with Watercress Salad** 134

**Pea Fusilli with Bacon
and Ricotta** 138

**Conchiglie with Spinach
and Goat Cheese** 196

**Goat Cheese and Sundried
Tomato Ravioli** 244

Veggie delights

Meat-free pasta dishes, perfect for entertaining or feeding the family.

Creamy Chickpea and Pasta Soup 28

Artichoke, Olive, and Lemon Linguine 30

Springtime Tortelloni with Ricotta 56

Chili and Caper Tagliatelle with Ciabatta Crumbs 78

Eggplant and Mozzarella Fusilli Lunghi 82

Tagliarelle with Pesto and Charred Tomatoes 162

Fresh Pasta Broth with Onion Garnish 180

Mushroom Tagliatelle Bolognese 194

Fusilli with Lentils, Kale, and Caramelized Onion 198

Pasta Primavera 208

Penne with Blackened Broccoli, Chili and Garlic 224

Creamy Asparagus Pasta 262

Meaty feasts

Delicious meals, perfect for a balanced meal.

Chorizo and Red Pepper Pasta 90

Chicken Fusilli with Red Pepper and Almond Pesto 104

Linguine with Spicy Lamb Sauce 118

Pasta with Pork and Mushrooms in a White Wine Sauce 122

Chicken Fettuccine Alfredo 144

Chicken Parmigiana with Tomato Fusilli Lunghi 152

Creamy Mustard and Sausage Pasta 154

Lamb Chops with Garlicky Zucchini and Anchovy Tagliatelle 246

Summery Sausage Pasta 250

Venison and Chestnut Gnocchetti Sardi 256

Mafaldine with Rich Confit Duck and Pancetta 260

Tagliarelle with Seared Steak and Goulash Sauce 276

QuickCook

Light
Bites

Recipes listed by cooking time

30

20

10

Zucchini, Pea, and Pasta Soup with Pesto

Serves 4

1 tablespoon olive oil
1 onion, finely chopped
3 tablespoons dry white wine
6 cups hot
   chicken stock
2 zucchini, chopped
⅔ cup frozen peas
4 oz macaroni
1½ tablespoons sour cream
4 tablespoons store-bought
   fresh green pesto
salt and pepper
crusty bread, to serve

- Heat the oil in a saucepan, add the onion, and cook for 5 minutes until softened. Pour over the wine and bring to a boil, then cook until reduced by half. Add the stock and simmer for 5 minutes.

- Add the zucchini and cook for 5 minutes, then stir in the peas and cook for an additional 2–3 minutes until tender.

- Meanwhile, cook the pasta in a large saucepan of salted boiling water according to the package instructions until al dente. Drain and add to the soup with the sour cream, then simmer for 1 minute.

- Ladle into serving bowls, then drizzle a spoonful of the pesto on top of each. Serve with plenty of crusty bread.

 Quick Zucchini, Pea, and Pasta Soup with Pesto Melt a little butter in a saucepan, add 3 chopped scallions and cook for a minute until softened. Pour over 6 cups hot chicken stock, then add 2 chopped zucchini and 4 oz farfalline pasta and simmer for about 5 minutes or until the pasta is cooked through. Add ⅔ cup frozen peas to the pan 2–3 minutes before the end of the cooking time and cook until tender. Serve drizzled with pesto as above.

 Zucchini, Pea, and Pasta Soup with Mint Pesto Toasts Make the soup as above. Meanwhile, lightly toast 3 tablespoons hazelnuts. Place in a small food processor or blender with ½ seeded and chopped chili and a handful of mint leaves. Add a good squeeze of lemon juice and a little grated zest and whiz together. Blend in enough extra virgin olive oil to form a smooth pesto. Toast 4 slices of ciabatta bread, then spoon on the pesto and crumble over 3 oz goat cheese. Ladle the soup into serving bowls and serve with the toasts on top.

Spaghetti with Beets and Goat Cheese

Serves 4

1 tablespoon butter
1 onion, finely sliced
1¼ cups chopped cooked beets,
½ cup dry white wine
¾ cup hot chicken or vegetable
  stock
14 oz spaghetti
3 oz firm goat cheese log, cut
  into 4 thick slices
5 tablespoons sour cream
salt and pepper
chopped dill weed, to garnish

· Heat the butter in a large saucepan, add the onion, and cook for 5 minutes or until softened. Add the beets and wine and cook for an additional 5 minutes or until the wine has reduced by half. Pour over the stock and simmer for 5 minutes.

· Meanwhile, cook the pasta in a large saucepan of salted boiling water according to the package instructions until al dente. Place the goat cheese slices on a baking sheet lined with foil. Cook under a preheated hot broiler for 3 minutes or until golden brown.

· Stir the sour cream into the beets and season with salt and pepper. Drain the pasta and spoon into serving bowls. Spoon over the beet sauce, top each with a slice of goat cheese, and serve sprinkled with dill.

---

10 Quick Beet and Goat Cheese Spaghetti Cook 14 oz spaghetti according to the package instructions until al dente. Meanwhile, place 1¼ cups chopped cooked beets and 4 oz soft goat cheese in a food processor or blender and whiz together to form a chunky sauce. Drain the pasta, reserving a little of the cooking water, and return to the pan. Stir through the sauce, adding a little cooking water to loosen, and serve with grated Parmesan cheese.

30 Beet Pasta Bites with Goat Cheese Cook 8 oz angel hair pasta according to the package instructions. Drain, then cool under cold running water and drain again. Grate 5 oz cooked beets into a large bowl, then mix together with the pasta and 1 beaten egg. Heat 1 tablespoon olive oil in a nonstick skillet. Spoon in tablespoons of the pasta mixture and cook for 2 minutes, then turn over and cook for an additional 2–3 minutes until golden. Remove from the pan and keep warm. Repeat with the rest of the mixture to make 8 pasta bites. Toss together 2 cups watercress, 1 tablespoon sherry vinegar, 3 tablespoons extra virgin olive oil, and the grated zest of ½ lemon in a bowl. Top the pasta cakes with the salad and serve with 3 oz soft goat cheese crumbled over.

3 Creamy Chickpea and Pasta Soup

Serves 4

2 tablespoons olive oil
1 onion, chopped
1 garlic clove, crushed
rosemary sprig, leaves stripped,
    or a pinch of dried rosemary
1 teaspoon tomato paste
pinch of dried red pepper flakes,
    plus extra to serve
2 x 13 oz cans chickpeas, rinsed
    and drained
6 cups hot chicken stock
5 oz conchigliette pasta
salt and pepper
chopped flat-leaf parsley,
    to garnish
Parmesan cheese shavings,
    to serve

- Heat the oil in a large saucepan, add the onion and garlic and cook for 5 minutes until softened. Stir in the rosemary, tomato paste and pepper flakes. Tip in the chickpeas, then add the stock and simmer for about 12 minutes. Remove the pan from the heat.

- Remove half the chickpeas from the pan using a slotted spoon. Using an immersion blender, whiz the remaining mixture to form a smooth soup and season with salt and pepper.

- Add the pasta and reserved chickpeas to the soup, return to the heat, and cook for an additional 5–7 minutes or until the pasta is cooked through.

- Ladle into serving bowls and serve sprinkled with the parsley, Parmesan shavings, and extra pepper flakes.

---

1 Quick Chickpea and Pasta Soup

Place 5 oz conchigliette, 2 rinsed and drained 13 oz cans chickpeas and 6 cups hot chicken stock in a large saucepan and simmer for 8 minutes until heated through and the pasta is cooked. Just before serving, stir in 5 tablespoons store-bought red pepper hummus, then sprinkle with plenty of chopped flat-leaf parsley.

2 Chickpea and Veggie Pasta Soup

with Rosemary Sauce Cook the onion and garlic as above, adding 1 chopped celery stick and 1 peeled and chopped carrot. Stir in the rosemary, tomato paste, pepper flakes, chickpeas, and stock as above and simmer for about 12 minutes. Add the conchigliette to the pan 7 minutes before the end of the cooking time. Meanwhile, place the stripped leaves from

2 rosemary sprigs, 1 small bunch of flat-leaf parsley, and 1 chopped garlic clove in a food processor or blender. Add a good squeeze of lemon juice and enough extra virgin olive oil to form a sauce. When the pasta is cooked through, ladle the soup into bowls and swirl over the rosemary sauce to serve.

Artichoke, Olive, and Lemon Linguine

Serves 4

11 oz linguine
1 cup char-grilled artichoke
    hearts in oil, drained
3 tablespoons extra virgin
    olive oil
juice and grated zest of 1 lemon
½ cup black olives
salt and pepper
chopped flat-leaf parsley,
    to garnish
Parmesan cheese shavings,
    to serve

- Cook the pasta in a large saucepan of salted boiling water according to the package instructions until al dente. Drain, reserving a little of the cooking water.

- Return the pasta to the pan and stir through the remaining ingredients, adding a little cooking water to loosen if needed, and season with salt and pepper.

- Spoon into serving bowls and serve sprinkled with the parsley and Parmesan shavings.

 Lemony Chicken, Artichoke, and Olive Linguine Heat a little olive oil in a skillet. Add 2 boneless chicken breasts and 4 chopped bacon slices and cook for 12–15 minutes, turning the chicken over once during cooking. Add 2 sliced scallions and 1 sliced garlic clove and cook for an additional 2 minutes until softened. Meanwhile, cook the linguine as above. Remove the chicken from the pan, discard the skin, and cut into bite-size pieces. Return to the pan and add the artichokes and black olives as above, a good squeeze of lemon juice, and 3 tablespoons sour cream and heat through. Drain the pasta and return to the pan. Stir through the chicken mixture with a handful of chopped flat-leaf parsley. Serve at once.

 Artichoke, Olive, and Lemon Frittata Cook 7 oz penne according to the package instructions until al dente. Drain, then cool slightly under cold running water and drain again. Return to the pan and toss together with 6 beaten eggs, 1 cup char-grilled artichoke hearts in oil, drained, and ½ cup black olives. Stir in a handful of chopped mint leaves and the grated zest of 1 lemon. Heat a little olive oil in a large skillet, pour in the egg mixture, and cook over a low heat for 15 minutes until just set (you may have to finish off under the broiler). Cut into wedges and serve.

30 Individual Bacon Pasta Frittatas

Serves 4

6 bacon slices
11 oz quick-cook spaghetti
5 eggs, beaten
½ cup light cream
½ cup grated Gruyère cheese
handful of flat-leaf parsley,
   chopped, to garnish
butter, for greasing
salt and pepper

- Cook the bacon under a preheated medium broiler for 7 minutes until cooked through. Cool, then cut into small pieces.

- Meanwhile, cook the pasta in a large saucepan of salted boiling water according to the package instructions until al dente. Drain, then cool under cold running water and drain again. Cut into 1 inch lengths.

- Mix together the eggs, cream, and most of the cheese in a large bowl and season well with salt and pepper. Stir in the cut pasta and bacon.

- Grease a 12-cup muffin pan. Spoon a little of the mixture into each cup until nearly to the top. Sprinkle with the remaining cheese, then place in a preheated oven, 400°F, for 15–20 minutes or until the mixture is just set. Serve sprinkled with parsley.

10 Simple Bacon Spaghetti with Toasted Bread Crumbs

Cook 4 bacon slices as above, then slice into small pieces. Meanwhile, cook the spaghetti as above. Heat a little olive oil in a skillet, add ½ cup fresh white bread crumbs and cook until crisp. Drain the pasta and return to the pan. Stir through the bacon, 3 tablespoons sour cream, and a handful of chopped basil leaves. Serve topped with the toasted bread crumbs.

20 Caramelized Onion and Prosciutto Spaghetti

Heat a little olive oil in a skillet, add 1 sliced onion and 1 sliced garlic clove, and cook over a low heat for 15–20 minutes until soft and golden. Meanwhile, cook the spaghetti as above. Drain well and return to the pan. Stir 2 tablespoons sour cream and 4 slices of prosciutto, cut into small strips, into the onions, then toss through the pasta. Serve immediately.

# 1 Penne with Broccoli and Blue Cheese Sauce

Serves 4

11 oz penne
1 small head of broccoli, broken
   into florets
5 oz creamy blue cheese, such as
   Gorgonzola or St Agur
3 tablespoons light cream
salt and pepper

- Cook the pasta in a large saucepan of salted boiling water according to the package instructions until al dente. Add the broccoli 5 minutes before the end of the cooking time and cook until tender.

- Meanwhile, place the cheese in a bowl and mash until smooth, then stir in the cream.

- Drain the pasta and broccoli, reserving a little of the cooking water, and return to the pan. Stir through the cheese mixture, adding a little cooking water to make a thin sauce if needed. Season well with salt and pepper and serve immediately.

2 **Broccoli and Ham Penne with Blue Cheese Sauce** Brush a little oil over 2 thick ham steaks and cook under a preheated medium broiler for 5–7 minutes on each side. Allow to cool, then slice. Meanwhile, make the recipe as above, stirring the sliced ham into the pasta with the cheese mixture. Serve immediately.

3 **Broccoli, Blue Cheese, and Penne Gratin** Cook 14 oz penne and the broccoli as above. Meanwhile, melt 3½ tablespoons butter in a saucepan and stir in ⅓ cup all-purpose flour to make a smooth paste. Cook until golden, then gradually whisk in 2 cups milk and simmer for 5–10 minutes until thickened. Stir through ⅔ cup chopped blue cheese. Drain the pasta and broccoli and mix together with the cheese sauce. Place in a heatproof dish and sprinkle with 1 cup grated mozzarella cheese. Cook under a preheated medium broiler for 5–10 minutes until golden and cooked through.

 # Spicy Fish Soup

Serves 4

2 tablespoons olive oil

1 garlic clove, sliced

1 red chili, seeded and finely chopped, plus extra sliced chili to serve (optional)

½ teaspoon ground cumin

1 teaspoon paprika

6 cups hot fish stock

14 oz white fish, such as cod or haddock, skinned, boned, and cut into bite-size chunks

5 oz stelline pasta

juice of ½ lemon

salt and pepper

cilantro sprigs, to garnish

- Heat the oil in a large saucepan, add the garlic and chili, and cook for 30 seconds until beginning to turn golden. Stir in the cumin and paprika, then pour over the stock.

- Bring to a boil, then reduce the heat, season with salt and pepper, add the fish and simmer for 5 minutes.

- Add the pasta and cook for an additional 7–10 minutes until the fish and pasta are cooked through.

- Ladle into serving bowls and drizzle over the lemon juice to taste. Serve with sprigs of cilantro and sliced chili, if desired.

 Tomato and Spicy Shrimp Soup Place 1¼ cups store-bought tomato pasta sauce and 3 cups hot fish stock in a saucepan and bring to a boil. Add the chili, spices, and stelline as above, then simmer for about 7 minutes until the pasta is cooked through. Add 5 oz cooked peeled shrimp to the pan 2 minutes before the end of the cooking time and cook until they are heated through. Serve immediately.

 Spicy Baked Fish with Herby Linguine Rub a little olive oil over 4 thick cod fillets or other white fish fillets, place in an ovenproof dish, and sprinkle with paprika and cumin. Allow to marinate for 5 minutes. Bake in a preheated oven, 375°F, for 10–15 minutes until cooked through. Mean-while, cook 10 oz linguine according to the package instructions until al dente. Drain, then cool under cold running water and drain again. Return to the pan and stir through 3 tablespoons extra virgin olive oil, a squeeze of lemon juice, 1 crushed garlic clove, and a handful of chopped mint and cilantro leaves. Serve alongside the baked fish.

Herby Fettuccine with Fried Eggs

Serves 4

10 oz fettuccine

2 tablespoons grated Parmesan
cheese, plus extra to serve

handful of flat-leaf parsley,
chopped, plus extra to garnish

3 tablespoons olive oil

1 garlic clove, finely chopped

4 eggs

pinch of dried red pepper flakes

salt and pepper

- Cook the pasta in a large saucepan of salted boiling water according to the package instructions until al dente. Drain, reserving a little of the cooking water, and return to the pan. Toss together with the Parmesan, parsley, and a little cooking water to loosen. Season well with salt and pepper.

- Meanwhile, heat the oil in a large nonstick skillet, add the garlic, and cook for a couple of seconds, then crack the eggs into the pan. Cook for 3 minutes so the whites are cooked through but the yolks are still runny.

- Spoon the pasta into serving bowls and top each with a fried egg. Serve sprinkled with the pepper flakes, extra chopped parsley and grated Parmesan.

 2 **Asparagus and Herb Fettuccine with Fried Eggs** Toss 5 oz trimmed asparagus spears in a little olive oil, then place on a broiler rack. Cook under a preheated hot broiler for 5 minutes until lightly charred, turning once, then cut into bite-size pieces. Cook and drain the fettuccine as above. Meanwhile, heat a little olive oil in a skillet and fry 4 quail eggs for 2 minutes until just cooked through. Toss the asparagus and a handful of chopped flat-leaf parsley through the pasta, then serve topped with the fried eggs and fresh Parmesan.

3 **Sausage, Fried Egg, and Herby Brunch Pasta** Heat a little olive oil in a large skillet, add 6 pork sausages, and cook over medium heat for 20 minutes or until cooked through. Remove the sausages from the pan, cool slightly, and cut into bite-size pieces. Add a handful of mushrooms, trimmed and halved, and cook for an additional 1–2 minutes, then add ½ cup cherry tomatoes and cook until the tomatoes start to soften. Meanwhile, cook the fettuccine and fry 4 eggs as above. Drain the pasta and toss together with the sausages, mushrooms, and tomatoes. Serve topped with a fried egg and sprinkled with chopped flat-leaf parsley and grated fresh Parmesan cheese.

Tagliatelle with Spicy Garlic Oil

Serves 4

½ cup extra virgin
   olive oil
2 garlic cloves, sliced
½ red chili, seeded if desired,
   and chopped
11 oz spinach and egg tagliatelle
salt and pepper
basil leaves, to garnish

- Pour the oil into a small saucepan, add the garlic, and cook over a very low heat for 7 minutes or until the garlic starts to turn golden (if it turns black, you'll need to start again). Remove from the heat and add the chili.

- Meanwhile, cook the pasta in a large saucepan of salted boiling water according to the package instructions until al dente.

- Drain the pasta, reserving a little of the cooking water. Whisk 2 tablespoons of the cooking water into the garlic and chili oil to make a smooth sauce, then season with salt and pepper and toss through the pasta, adding a little more water if needed.

- Spoon onto serving plates and serve sprinkled with basil leaves.

2 Tagliatelle with Roasted Garlic

Sauce Place 8 garlic cloves, unpeeled, in a small roasting pan and toss in 2 tablespoons olive oil. Place in a preheated oven, 325°F, for about 15 minutes or until soft. Squeeze the garlic out of their skins and mash together with 3 tablespoons sour cream in a bowl. Meanwhile, cook and drain the tagliatelle as above. Stir through the garlic sauce, adding a little cooking water to loosen if needed, and serve sprinkled with grated Parmesan cheese.

3 Garlicky Onion Tagliatelle

Heat a little olive oil in a skillet, add 1 sliced onion, and cook over a low heat for 20–25 minutes until softened and browned. Meanwhile, heat a knob of butter in a saucepan, add 3 sliced garlic cloves, 1 trimmed, cleaned and sliced leek, 1 sliced red onion, and 3 sliced scallions and cook gently for about 5 minutes until softened. Pour over 5 tablespoons chicken stock and bubble for 5 minutes until the liquid has nearly cooked away. Meanwhile, cook and drain the tagliatelle as above. Toss through the garlicky onion mixture and the browned onion, then serve sprinkled with chopped chives and grated Pecorino cheese.

Pasta Cakes with Scrambled Eggs and Salmon

Serves 4

10 oz angel hair pasta
6 tablespoons olive oil
4 eggs
3 tablespoons mascarpone
cheese
handful of grated Parmesan
cheese
4 slices of smoked salmon, cut
into thin strips
salt and pepper
thinly sliced chives, to garnish

- Cook the pasta in a large saucepan of salted boiling water according to the package instructions. Drain, then cool under cold running water and drain again. Tip into a bowl and toss through 1 teaspoon of the oil. Lightly beat 1 egg in a bowl and then mix together with the pasta.

- Heat a large nonstick skillet, add half the remaining oil, and curl the pasta into small cakes about 1 inch wide. Add about 4 of the pasta cakes to the pan and cook for 2 minutes, flattening the cakes down with the back of a spoon. Turn the cakes over and cook for 1 minute more until golden all over. Remove from the pan and keep warm. Repeat with the remaining pasta cakes to make about 12.

- Crack the remaining 3 eggs into a small skillet, dollop over the mascarpone and season well. Place over low heat and cook for a couple of minutes until just beginning to set, then cook, gently stirring, for 3–5 minutes until creamy. Add the Parmesan and season well. Place 3 pasta cakes on each serving plate, spoon over a little scrambled egg, and top with strips of smoked salmon. Serve sprinkled with chives.

 Easy Salmon Carbonara Cook 14 oz angel hair pasta as above. Meanwhile, mix 2 tablespoons mascarpone and 1 beaten egg in a bowl. Drain the pasta, reserving a little of the cooking water, and return to the pan. Stir through the egg mixture and 4 slices of smoked salmon, cut into strips, adding a little cooking water to loosen if needed. Serve with extra mascarpone dolloped on top and sprinkled with chives as above.

 Pan-Fried Salmon with Creamy Asparagus Pasta Place the juice and grated zest of 1 lemon, 1 cup dry white wine, and 1 bay leaf in a saucepan and bubble over medium heat for 5–10 minutes until reduced. Pour in 1 cup heavy cream and cook for an additional 5–10 minutes until reduced by half. Keep warm. Gzest plenty of black pepper over 4 thin salmon steaks. Heat a little olive oil in a large skillet, add the salmon, and cook for 5 minutes on each side or until the fish is cooked and flakes easily. Meanwhile, cook 10 oz linguine according to the package instructions until al dente. Add 5 oz asparagus tips to the pan 3 minutes before the end of the cooking time and cook until tender. Pass the sauce through a sieve, then season and mix in 1 egg yolk and a handful of chopped chives. Drain the pasta and asparagus and return to the pan. Stir through the sauce and serve alongside the salmon.

3 Greek-Style Tomato, Olive, and Feta Pasta Salad

Serves 4

1 cup cherry tomatoes, halved

4 tablespoons extra virgin
  olive oil

1½ tablespoons white
  wine vinegar

1 teaspoon oregano leaves,
  plus extra to garnish

1 teaspoon sugar

8 oz penne

¼ cucumber, diced

½ cup small black olives

3 oz feta cheese, crumbled

salt and pepper

- Mix together the tomatoes and 2 tablespoons of the oil in a bowl, then place on a baking sheet. Drizzle over 1 tablespoon of the vinegar, sprinkle with the oregano and sugar, and season well with salt and pepper. Place in a preheated oven, 325°F, for 20 minutes or until soft and starting to shrivel. Allow to cool slightly.

- Meanwhile, cook the pasta in a large saucepan of salted boiling water according to the package instructions until al dente. Drain, then cool under cold running water and drain again. Tip into a serving dish and stir through the remaining oil and vinegar.

- Gently stir in the cucumber, olives, and cooked tomatoes. Toss together and add the feta. Serve sprinkled with extra oregano leaves.

 Quick Olive, Arugula, and Feta Pasta Salad Cook 10 oz fresh penne according to the package instructions until al dente, then drain as above. Tip into a serving dish and toss together with 2 cups arugula leaves, ½ cup pitted black olives, a squeeze of lemon juice, and 1 tablespoon extra virgin olive oil. Serve sprinkled with 3 oz crumbled feta cheese.

 Olive and Tomato Penne with Baked Feta Heat a little olive oil in a saucepan, add 1 chopped onion and 2 finely chopped garlic cloves, and cook until softened. Add ½ cup pitted black olives and fry for 1–2 minutes more. Stir in a 13 oz can cherry tomatoes and bring to a boil. Reduce the heat, then simmer for 12 minutes until the sauce has thickened. Meanwhile, cook 10 oz penne as above. Place 7 oz feta cheese, in one piece, on a sheet of foil. Drizzle with olive oil and sprinkle with 1 teaspoon oregano leaves. Fold over the foil to make a packet and place on a baking sheet. Bake in a preheated oven, 400°F, for 10 minutes or until soft. Remove from the foil and cut into large pieces. Drain the pasta and return to the pan. Stir through the tomato sauce and serve topped with the baked cheese.

1 Herby Goat Cheese Pasta

Serves 4

11 oz fresh reginette pasta

5 oz soft goat cheese

handful of basil leaves, chopped, plus extra leaves to serve (optional)

handful of flat-leaf parsley, chopped, plus extra leaves to serve (optional)

handful of mint leaves, chopped, plus extra leaves to serve (optional)

salt and pepper

- Cook the pasta in a large saucepan of salted boiling water according to the package instructions until al dente.

- Meanwhile, mash together the goat cheese and herbs in a bowl and season lightly with salt and pepper.

- Drain the pasta, reserving a little of the cooking water, and return to the pan. Stir through the herby cheese mixture, adding a little cooking water to loosen if needed. Spoon into bowls and serve sprinkled with extra herb leaves, if desired.

 Herby Goat Cheese Pasta with Garlicky Bread Crumbs Place 2 oz ciabatta bread in a food processor or blender and whiz to form bread crumbs. Transfer to a bowl and toss together with 2 tablespoons olive oil and 1 crushed garlic clove. Tip onto a baking sheet and cook under a preheated broiler for a couple of minutes, turning often, until golden all over. Make the recipe as above, then serve sprinkled with the garlicky bread crumbs.

 Tomato and Basil Pasta with Goat Cheese Heat 2 tablespoons olive oil in a saucepan, add 3 sliced garlic cloves, and cook until softened. Tip in 2 x 13 oz cans chopped tomatoes and simmer for 25 minutes until the sauce is very thick. Season well, then stir through a handful of chopped basil leaves. Meanwhile, cook and drain the reginette as above. Stir in the tomato and basil sauce and serve with 5 oz soft goat cheese crumbled on top.

 # Salmon Pasta Salad with Dill Dressing

Serves 4

12 oz fresh fusilli
2 scallions, sliced
¼ cucumber, chopped
5 oz smoked salmon,
   cut into strips

For the dill dressing

⅓ cup sour cream
4 tablespoons mayonnaise
handful of dill weed, finely
   chopped
salt and pepper

- Cook the pasta in a large saucepan of salted boiling water according to the package instructions until al dente. Drain the pasta, then cool under cold running water and drain again.

- Meanwhile, to make the dill dressing, mix together the sour cream, mayonnaise, and dill in a bowl and season with salt and pepper.

- Tip the pasta into a serving dish and stir through the scallions, cucumber, smoked salmon, and dill dressing.

 Summery Poached Salmon and Dill Pasta Cut 1 fennel bulb into slices and place in a saucepan with a 14 oz piece of salmon fillet. Pour over 6 tablespoons dry white wine, enough fish stock to cover, and a couple of dill sprigs. Bring to a boil and then simmer for 10–12 minutes until the fish is cooked through and flakes easily. Remove the fish and fennel with a slotted spoon. Flake the fish into large chunks, removing any skin and bones, and keep warm with the fennel. Boil the poaching liquid until reduced down to 5 tablespoons, then stir through 3 tablespoons sour cream. Meanwhile, cook and drain the fusilli as above. Stir through the sauce, fennel, and salmon. Sprinkle with a little chopped dill and serve immediately.

Salmon and Dill Frittata Cook 10 oz spaghetti according to package instructions until al dente. Drain, then cool under cold running water and drain again. Tip into a large bowl and mix together with 6 eggs, 5 oz smoked salmon, cut into strips, and a good handful of chopped dill. Heat a skillet, add 3 tablespoons olive oil, and tip in the pasta mixture. Cook over low heat for 15 minutes or until set. Cut into wedges, then serve dolloped with mascarpone cheese and sprinkled with extra chopped dill.

20 Fresh Herb Pasta Salad

Serves 4

7 oz orzo
5 tablespoons extra virgin
   olive oil
juice of ½ lemon
2 scallions, chopped
¼ cucumber, finely chopped
½ cup chopped tomatoes
large handful of flat-leaf parsley,
   chopped
small handful of mint leaves,
   chopped
salt and pepper

- Cook the pasta in a large saucepan of salted boiling water according to the package instructions. Drain, then cool under cold running water and drain again.

- Tip into a serving dish and stir in the oil and lemon juice and season well with salt and pepper. Toss through the remaining ingredients and serve.

10 Simple Herby Pasta Cook the orzo as above. Drain and return to the pan. Stir in 2 tablespoons butter, the chopped herbs as above, and a squeeze of lemon juice. Serve immediately.

30 Fresh Herb Pasta Salad Middle-Eastern Style Make the pasta salad as above, adding a handful of pitted black olives, and arrange on a bed of chopped romaine lettuce. Cut 2 round pita breads in half horizontally (so they are very thin), then cut into wedges and place on a baking sheet. Drizzle with olive oil and sprinkle over paprika. Place in a preheated oven, 375°F, for 5–10 minutes until just crisp. Allow to cool before sprinkling over the salad to serve.

1 Spicy Mushroom Rigatoni Bake

Serves 2

10 oz fresh rigatoni

2 tablespoons olive oil

1 garlic clove, finely sliced

½ red chili, seeded if desired, and chopped

5 oz mixed mushrooms, preferably wild, trimmed and halved if large

grated zest of 1 lemon

handful of flat-leaf parsley, chopped

salt and pepper

grated Parmesan cheese, to serve

- Cook the pasta in a large saucepan of salted boiling water according to the package instructions until al dente.

- Meanwhile, heat the oil in a skillet, add the garlic, chili, and mushrooms and cook for a couple of minutes until the mushrooms brown slightly. Season well with salt and pepper.

- Drain the pasta and return to the pan. Toss through the mushroom mixture and most of the lemon zest and parsley, reserving some for garnish.

- Place in a preheated oven, 400°F, for 15 minutes or until golden, bubbling, and cooked through.

- To serve, sprinkle with the reserved lemon zest and parsley followed by the Parmesan.

---

2 Rigatoni with Baked Mushrooms

Place 4 trimmed field mushrooms in an ovenproof baking dish. Dot over 2 tablespoons butter, season well, and sprinkle with the leaves stripped from 1 thyme sprig. Place in a preheated oven, 350°F, for 15 minutes. Remove from the oven and chop the mushrooms. Meanwhile, cook 7 oz dried rigatoni according to the package instructions until al dente. Drain and return to the pan, then stir through the chopped mushrooms with a squeeze of lemon juice. Serve immediately.

3 Rigatoni with Mushroom and Blue Cheese Sauce

Heat a knob of butter and 1 tablespoon olive oil in a skillet, add ½ thickly sliced onion, and gently cook for 20 minutes until completely softened. Add 3 oz mixed wild mushrooms, trimmed and halved if large, and cook for 3–5 minutes more until softened. Mash 2½ oz Gorgonzola in a bowl until smooth and stir into the onion and mushrooms. Pour in 3 tablespoons heavy cream and heat through. Meanwhile, cook 7 oz dried rigatoni according to the package instructions until al dente. Drain and return to the pan, then stir through the sauce and serve sprinkled with chopped flat-leaf parsley.

Creamy Walnut Orecchiette

Serves 4

10 oz fresh orecchiette pasta
salt and pepper
chopped basil leaves, to garnish

For the walnut paste

1 ⅓ cups walnuts
3 tablespoons heavy cream
1 garlic clove, crushed
¼ cup grated Parmesan cheese,
   plus extra to serve

- Cook the pasta in a large saucepan of salted boiling water according to the package instructions until al dente.

- Meanwhile, make the walnut paste. Place the walnuts in a skillet and dry-fry for a couple of minutes, shaking the pan every now and again, until toasted. Reserve some of the nuts for garnish and place the remainder in a food processor or blender. Add the cream, garlic, and Parmesan, then whiz together to form a smooth paste.

- Drain the pasta, reserving a little of the cooking water, and return to the pan. Stir in the walnut paste, adding a little cooking water to loosen if needed. Season well with salt and pepper.

- Spoon into serving bowls and serve sprinkled with the reserved walnuts, basil, and extra Parmesan.

2 **Walnut and Arugula Orecchiette** Put 3 oz ciabatta bread in a food processor or blender and whiz to form bread crumbs. Soak half the bread crumbs in the 3 tablespoons heavy cream for 5–10 minutes to soften. Make the walnut paste as above, adding the soaked bread crumbs. Toss the remaining bread crumbs in a little olive oil and toast in a skillet until crisp. Meanwhile, cook and drain the orecchiette as above. Stir in the walnut sauce, adding a little cooking water to loosen if needed. Season, stir in a handful of arugula leaves and top with crispy bread crumbs.

3 **Crispy Chicken and Walnut Orecchiette** Cook 10 oz dried orecchiette according to the package instructions until al dente. Make the walnut paste as above, adding 5 tablespoons chicken stock to form a thin sauce. Pour into a large saucepan and heat through. Tear 2 store-bought roasted chicken breasts into strips, discarding the skin, and stir through the sauce. Drain the pasta and stir into the sauce with 2 sliced scallions, a pinch of paprika, and a little chopped dill weed. Tip into a large heatproof dish. Cover with 1 cup fresh white bread crumbs, drizzle with olive oil, and cook under a preheated medium broiler for 5–10 minutes or until cooked through.

 # Springtime Tortelloni with Ricotta

Serves 2

8 oz pack spinach and ricotta
  tortelloni
½ cup frozen fava beans
½ cup frozen peas
grated zest of 1 lemon
1 tablespoon extra virgin olive oil
¼ cup ricotta cheese
salt
handful of mint leaves, chopped,
  to garnish

- Cook the pasta in a large saucepan of salted boiling water according to the package instructions. Add the fava beans 3–4 minutes and the peas 2–3 minutes before the end of the cooking time and cook until tender. Drain the pasta and vegetables and return to the pan.

- Stir through the lemon zest and olive oil. Spoon into serving bowls and serve topped with the ricotta and mint.

 Tortelloni with Pancetta and Ricotta Heat a little olive oil in a skillet, add 2 sliced scallions and cook until softened. Add 3½ oz pancetta cubes and cook gently for 7–10 minutes until lightly browned, then stir in a splash of dry white wine and cook until reduced down. Meanwhile, cook and drain the tortelloni as above. Stir through the pancetta and serve topped with the ricotta and mint as above.

 Tomato and Ricotta Tortelloni Bake Cook 8 oz tortelloni for 1 minute less than directed on the package instructions. Drain well and arrange half over the bottom of an ovenproof dish. Pour over 5 tablespoons store-bought tomato pasta sauce, then sprinkle with ¼ cup ricotta cheese. Add another layer of tortelloni and tomato sauce. Top with ⅓ cup ricotta cheese, 2 oz sliced mozzarella cheese, and a small handful of grated Parmesan cheese. Place in a preheated oven, 375°F, for 15–20 minutes until golden and heated through.

PAS-LITE-SOJ

Bacon and Tomato Tortiglioni with Mascarpone Mayonnaise

Serves 4

1 tablespoon olive oil
4 bacon slices
5 oz cherry tomatoes
on the vine
11 oz tortiglioni
1¼ cups arugula leaves

For the mascarpone mayonnaise

1 egg yolk
½ cup mascarpone cheese
3 tablespoons extra virgin
olive oil
2 tablespoons grated
Parmesan cheese
salt and pepper

- Rub the oil onto a broiler pan, add the bacon, and cook under a preheated medium broiler for 5–7 minutes until starting to crisp. Add the tomatoes. Shake the pan to coat in the oil, season, and return to the broiler. Cook for 5 minutes or until the bacon is cooked and tomatoes are lightly charred. Meanwhile, cook the pasta in a saucepan of salted boiling water according to the package instructions until al dente.

- To make the mascarpone mayonnaise, place the egg yolk and mascarpone in a food processor and whiz together. With the motor still running, add the oil through the funnel, one small drop at a time, until you get a smooth mayonnaise-like sauce. Stir in the Parmesan and season.

- Drain the pasta, reserving a little cooking water, and return to the pan. Stir through a little of the mascarpone mixture, followed by the arugula. Add a little cooking water to loosen if needed. Spoon into bowls, dollop over the remaining mayonnaise and top with the bacon slices and tomato.

Quick Tomato, Prosciutto and Arugula Spaghettini Cook 11 oz spaghettini in a large saucepan of salted boiling water according to the package instructions until al dente. Drain, then return to the pan. Stir through 3 tablespoons mascarpone cheese mixed with 2 tablespoons grated Parmesan cheese, 4 drained and chopped sundried tomatoes in oil, and 4 slices of prosciutto, cut into strips. Serve sprinkled with plenty of chopped arugula leaves.

Bacon, Tomato, and Arugula Pasta Soufflés Cook the bacon as above. Meanwhile, cook 8 oz quick-cook spaghetti according to the package instructions until al dente. Melt 2 tablespoons butter in a large saucepan and stir in ¼ cup all-purpose flour to make a smooth paste. Cook until golden, then gradually whisk in 1¼ cups milk and simmer, stirring regularly, for 5 minutes until thickened. Lift off the heat and stir through ¼ cup grated Parmesan cheese and 3 egg yolks. Whisk 3 egg whites in a clean bowl until stiff peaks form. Drain the pasta, slice into 1 inch lengths and chop the bacon, then add to the cheese sauce with 2 drained and chopped sundried tomatoes and a handful of arugula leaves, finely chopped. Gently stir in the whisked egg whites in three stages. Spoon into 4 individual greased soufflé dishes and place in a preheated oven, 400°F, for 20 minutes or until golden and just cooked through.

 # Pasta Puttanesca

Serves 4

3 tablespoons olive oil

2 garlic cloves, sliced

½ teaspoon dried red pepper flakes

8 anchovy fillets in oil, drained

2 x 13 oz cans chopped tomatoes

⅔ cup black olives

1 tablespoon capers, rinsed and drained

10 oz pappardelle

salt and pepper

torn basil leaves, to garnish

- Heat the oil in a large saucepan, add the garlic, red pepper flakes, and anchovies and cook, stirring frequently, for a couple of minutes until the anchovies begin to disintegrate.

- Stir in the tomatoes and cook, fairly vigorously, for 15 minutes or until the sauce has thickened. Add the olives and capers and season with salt and pepper.

- Meanwhile, cook the pasta in a large saucepan of salted boiling water according to the package instructions until al dente. Drain and toss through the sauce.

- Spoon into serving bowls and serve sprinkled with the basil.

 Pappardelle with a No-Cook Caper and Olive Sauce Cook and drain the pappardelle as above. Meanwhile, mix together 1 crushed garlic clove and 3 tablespoons extra virgin olive oil in a bowl. Roughly chop 1 large tomato and stir into the dressing with 2 teaspoons rinsed and drained capers and a handful of pitted black olives. Drain the pasta and return to the pan. Stir through the sauce and serve immediately.

 Chicken Pappardelle with Caper and Olive Dressing Cook 4 boneless chicken breasts under a preheated hot broiler for 7 minutes on each side or until golden and cooked through. Cook and drain the pappardelle as above, then stir through 1½ cups store-bought tomato pasta sauce. Heat 3 tablespoons olive oil in a small skillet, add a handful of pitted black olives, and cook for 1–2 minutes until beginning to sizzle. Add 1 tablespoon rinsed and drained capers and cook for 30 seconds. Stir in 2 tablespoons chopped flat-leaf parsley and a squeeze of lemon juice. Arrange the pasta and slice and arrange the chicken on serving plates. Spoon over the warm dressing and serve.

Creamy Chicken and Artichoke Frittata

Serves 4

11 oz spaghetti
6 eggs
6 tablespoons sour cream
2 store-bought roasted chicken
  breasts
¼ cup grated Parmesan cheese
1½ cups artichoke hearts in oil or
  brine, drained and cut into
  wedges
2 scallions, sliced
handful of basil leaves, chopped
small handful of mint leaves,
  chopped
2 tablespoons olive oil
salt and pepper

- Cook the pasta in a saucepan of salted boiling water according to the package instructions until al dente.

- Meanwhile, whisk together the eggs and sour cream in a large bowl and season well with salt and pepper. Tear the chicken into shreds, discarding the skin, and mix in with the Parmesan, artichokes, scallions, basil, and mint.

- Drain the pasta, then cool slightly under cold running water and drain again. Mix together with the egg mixture and season well.

- Heat a large nonstick skillet over medium heat, then add the oil. Tip in the pasta mixture, smoothing over the surface with a spoon. Allow to cook over a medium heat for 20 minutes until just set. Serve cut into wedges.

 Quick Chicken and Artichoke Spaghetti Cook the spaghetti as above. Meanwhile, tear the chicken breasts into shreds as above and quarter the artichoke hearts. Drain the pasta, reserve a little of the cooking water, and return to the pan. Stir through the chicken, artichokes, a dollop of mascarpone cheese, and a handful of grated Parmesan cheese, adding a little cooking water to loosen if needed. Serve at once.

Griddled Chicken and Artichoke Pasta Salad Season 2 boneless chicken breasts and cook on a preheated hot griddle for 7 minutes on each side or until cooked through. Meanwhile, cook 10 oz fusilli according to the package instructions until al dente. Drain, then cool under cold running water and drain again. Tip into a serving dish and toss together with the juice of ½ lemon and 3 tablespoons extra virgin olive oil. Tear the chicken into shreds, discarding the skin, and mix into the salad with the artichoke hearts as above, cut into chunks, and a handful of chopped mint leaves.

30 Red Pepper, Arugula, and Parmesan Pasta Salad

Serves 4

4 tablespoons extra virgin
   olive oil
1 garlic clove, finely chopped
1 red chili, seeded and
   finely chopped
4 red bell peppers, cored, seeded,
   and cut into wedges
11 oz gigli pasta
1 tablespoon white balsamic
   vinegar
2 cups arugula leaves
handful of Parmesan cheese
   shavings
salt and pepper

- Heat 2 tablespoons of the olive oil in a skillet, add the garlic and chili and cook for 30 seconds. Add the bell peppers and cook over low heat for 20–25 minutes or until very soft. Allow to cool slightly.

- Meanwhile, cook the pasta in a large saucepan of salted boiling water according to the package instructions until al dente. Drain, then rinse under cold running water until warm and drain again. Tip into a serving dish.

- Toss through the remaining oil, balsamic vinegar, arugula, and the red peppers with all their cooking juices and season with salt and pepper. Serve sprinkled with the Parmesan.

1 Pasta with Quick Roasted Red Pepper Sauce

Cook and drain the gigli as above. Meanwhile, place 2 drained roasted red peppers from a jar, 1 crushed garlic clove, and ½ cup ricotta cheese in a food processor or blender and whiz together to form a creamy sauce. Drain the pasta, reserving a little of the cooking water, and return to the pan. Stir through the red pepper sauce, adding a little cooking water to loosen if needed, and a handful of chopped basil leaves. Serve immediately.

2 Spicy Red Pepper Pasta

Cut 4 cored and seeded red bell peppers into thin strips. Heat a little olive oil in a skillet, add the red pepper strips, and cook gently for 15 minutes until softened. Meanwhile, cook and drain the gigli as above. Place 3 seeded tomatoes, 1 chopped scallion, and 1 halved and seeded red chili in a food processor or blender and whiz together to form a chunky sauce. Drain the pasta and return to the pan. Stir through the tomato sauce, 3 tablespoons olive oil, and the cooked peppers. Serve immediately.

Fusilli Amatriciana with Pancetta

Serves 4

2 tablespoons olive oil

1 red chili, seeded if desired, and finely chopped

8 oz pancetta slices, cut into strips

1 onion, finely chopped

1 rosemary sprig, leaves stripped and chopped

6 tablespoons fruity red wine

13 oz can chopped tomatoes

¾ cup water

14 oz fusilli

salt and pepper

grated Parmesan cheese, to serve

- Heat a skillet until hot, add the oil, chili, and pancetta and cook until beginning to crisp. Add the onion and rosemary and cook for an additional 3–5 minutes until lightly browned.

- Pour over the wine and bubble until reduced by half, then add the tomatoes and the measurement water and allow to simmer for at least 20 minutes until thickened. Season well with salt and pepper.

- Meanwhile, cook the pasta in a large saucepan of salted boiling water according to the package instructions until al dente. Drain and return to the pan, then toss through the sauce.

- Spoon into serving bowls and serve sprinkled with the Parmesan cheese.

Fusilli with Prosciutto and Cherry Tomatoes Cook and drain the fusilli as above. Toss through 10 halved cherry tomatoes, a squeeze of lemon juice, 2 tablespoons sour cream and 4 oz thinly sliced prosciutto, cut into small strips. Serve immediately.

Bacon and Sundried Tomato Fusilli Heat a little butter in a skillet, add 1 trimmed, cleaned, and sliced leek and cook for 5 minutes until beginning to soften. Cut 4 bacon slices into small strips, add to the pan with 2 sliced scallions, and cook for an additional 5 minutes. Pour over 1½ tablespoons dry white wine and cook for 3 minutes until reduced. Stir in 3 drained and chopped sundried tomatoes in oil and 4 tablespoons sour cream. Meanwhile, cook and drain the fusilli as above, then toss through the sauce. Serve at once.

1⏲ Spaghettini with Tomato and Basil Butter

Serves 4

5 tablespoons butter, softened

5 sunblush tomatoes in oil,
   drained and finely chopped

handful of basil leaves, finely
   chopped,

grated zest of 1 lemon

11 oz spaghettini

salt

- Mix together the butter, sunblush tomatoes, basil, and lemon zest in a bowl and season well with salt and pepper. Place on a sheet of plastic wrap and roll up tightly to form a cylinder. Place in the freezer for 5 minutes to firm. (You can also make this ahead of time and store in the refrigerator or freezer until ready to use.)

- Meanwhile, cook the pasta in a large saucepan of salted boiling water according to the package instructions until al dente. Drain well and pile onto serving plates.

- Cut slices of the flavored butter, place on top of the pasta, and serve immediately.

2⏲ Tomato and Basil Spaghettini with a Buttery Sauce

Heat a little butter in a saucepan, add 1 finely chopped shallot, and cook for a couple of minutes until softened. Pour over ⅔ cup dry white wine and cook for about 10 minutes until reduced. Cut 2 tablespoons cold butter into small chunks and whisk into the sauce one chunk at a time. Meanwhile, cook and drain the spaghettini as above. Stir through a handful of drained and chopped sunblush tomatoes in oil and a handful of chopped basil leaves and serve with the buttery sauce drizzled over.

3⏲ Spaghettini with Slow-Cooked Tomatoes and Basil

Cut 20 small tomatoes in half and arrange on a baking sheet. Drizzle over 3 tablespoons olive oil, 1 tablespoon balsamic vinegar, and 1 teaspoon sugar. Place in a preheated oven, 325°F, for 25–30 minutes until softened and lightly browned. Meanwhile, cook and drain the spaghettini as above. Toss through the tomatoes, a little more balsamic vinegar, a knob of butter, and a handful of basil leaves and serve with 4 oz soft goat cheese crumbled over.

Tuna and White Bean Pasta with Gremolata

Serves 4

5 tablespoons light cream
13 oz can cannellini beans, rinsed
and drained
7½ oz can tuna in oil, drained
11 oz ferretto pasta
salt

For the gremolata

1 garlic clove
grated zest of 1 lemon
handful of flat-leaf parsley,
chopped

- Place the cream and beans in a saucepan and cook for 15 minutes or until the beans are very soft, adding a little water if needed. Stir the tuna into the sauce.

- Meanwhile, cook the pasta in a large saucepan of salted boiling water according to the package instructions until al dente.

- To make the gremolata, place the garlic, lemon zest, and parsley on a board and chop until fine but not mushy.

- Drain the pasta, reserving a little of the cooking water. Mix together the pasta and tuna sauce, adding a little cooking water to loosen if needed.

- Spoon into serving bowls and serve sprinkled with the gremolata.

 Quick Tuna and White Bean Penne

Cook 14 oz fresh penne according to the package instructions until al dente. Add the cannellini beans as above to the pan 2 minutes before the end of the cooking time. Drain and return to the pan. Stir through 2 tablespoons sour cream, the grated zest of 1 lemon, the tuna as above, and a handful of chopped flat-leaf parsley. Serve immediately.

Griddled Tuna with Creamy White Bean Pasta Heat a little olive oil in a saucepan, add 1 chopped onion and 1 crushed garlic clove, and cook until softened. Add the cannellini beans and cream as above and a strip of orange and lemon zest and simmer for 15 minutes until really soft and creamy. Remove the zest and season with salt and pepper. Meanwhile, cook and drain the ferretto as above, then add to the beans. Rub a little black pepper and olive oil over 4 tuna steaks. Heat a griddle pan until smoking, add the tuna and cook for 3–5 minutes on each side or until browned on the outside but still rare inside. Spoon the creamy bean pasta into bowls, place the steaks on top, and serve sprinkled with chopped flat-leaf parsley.

QuickCook
Midweek Meals

Recipes listed by cooking time

30

20

Creamy Asparagus, Pea, and Lemon Pasta

Serves 4

1 lb fresh cavatappi pasta
⅔ cup frozen peas
5 oz thin asparagus tips
juice and grated zest of 1 lemon
½ cup mascarpone cheese
2 tablespoons extra virgin
   olive oil
salt and pepper
chopped basil leaves, to garnish

- Cook the pasta in a large saucepan of salted boiling water according to the package instructions until al dente. Add the peas and asparagus 3 minutes before the end of the cooking time and cook until tender.

- Meanwhile, mix together most of the grated lemon zest and the mascarpone in a bowl.

- Drain the pasta and vegetables, reserving a little of the cooking water. Set aside the asparagus and keep warm, and return the pasta and peas to the pan. Stir through the lemon juice and oil, loosening with a little cooking water.

- Season well and spoon into serving bowls. Sprinkle with the basil and the rest of the zest, top with the asparagus, and serve with a dollop of the lemon mascarpone in each dish.

20 Asparagus and Pea Spirali with

Lemon Sauce Cook 14 oz spirali according to the instructions until al dente, adding the vegetables to the pan as above. Meanwhile, melt 2 tablespoons butter in a saucepan and stir in 3 tablespoons all-purpose flour to make a smooth paste. Cook until golden, then gradually whisk in 6 tablespoons milk and 6 tablespoons heavy cream. Simmer for 5 minutes until thickened, then stir through the grated zest of 1 lemon and a handful of chopped basil leaves. Drain the pasta and vegetables and return to the pan, then stir through the sauce. Serve at once.

30 Asparagus, Pea, and Lemon Spirali

en Papillote Cook 14 oz spirali for 2 minutes less than directed on the package instructions, adding the vegetables to the pan as above, then drain. Cut out 4 large pieces of nonstick parchment paper and divide the drained pasta and vegetables between them. Squeeze over the juice of 1 lemon and pour over 3 tablespoons hot chicken stock. Fold over the parchment paper to seal the packets and place on a baking sheet. Place in a preheated oven, 350°F, for 10 minutes or until heated through. Open the packets, spoon 1 tablespoon mascarpone cheese over each, and serve

topped with a slice of Taleggio cheese.

Chili and Caper Tagliatelle with Ciabatta Crumbs

Serves 4

3 slices of ciabatta bread
5 tablespoons olive oil
4 garlic cloves
1 red chili, seeded if desired, and finely sliced
2 tablespoons capers, rinsed and drained
14 oz tagliatelle
juice and grated zest of 1 lemon
salt and pepper

- Place the ciabatta in a small food processor or blender and whiz to form coarse bread crumbs. Pour the oil into a small skillet and add the garlic. Cook over low heat for about 10 minutes until a deep golden color, then remove the cloves with a slotted spoon and discard. Add the bread crumbs to the pan and cook for an additional couple of minutes until beginning to brown. Remove the bread crumbs with a slotted spoon and set aside. Add the chili and capers and cook for 2 minutes until lightly browned.

- Meanwhile, cook the pasta in a large saucepan of salted boiling water according to the package instructions until al dente. Drain, reserving a little of the cooking water, and return to the pan. Stir in the flavored oil, lemon zest and juice, and a little cooking water if needed. Season well with salt and pepper.

- Spoon into serving bowls and serve sprinkled with the bread crumbs.

1 — Easy Chili, Caper, and Tomato Tagliatelle

Tagliatelle Cook and drain the tagliatelle as above and toss with the chili and capers as above, 3 drained and chopped sunblush tomatoes in oil, and ½ cup halved cherry tomatoes. Add a squeeze of lemon juice and top with plenty of arugula leaves. Serve immediately.

3 — Chili and Caper Tagliatelle Packets with Crispy Bread Crumbs

Cook the tagliatelle for 2 minutes less than directed on the package instructions. Drain well and divide between 4 large squares of foil. Mix together a squeeze of lemon juice, 1 crushed garlic clove, and the olive oil, chili, and capers as above and spoon over the pasta. Lift up the edges of the foil and fold over to seal, then place on a baking sheet. Cook in a preheated oven, 350°F, for 10 minutes or until cooked through. Whiz the ciabatta slices as above to make bread crumbs, then toss in a little olive oil and toast in a skillet until crisp. Tear open the packets with a knife and sprinkle over a handful of chopped basil leaves. Dollop over a little sour cream and sprinkle with the crispy bread crumbs. Serve immediately.

 # Spaghetti with Watercress Pesto and Blue Cheese

Serves 2

7 oz whole-wheat spaghetti
2 oz blue cheese, thickly sliced
salt and pepper

For the watercress pesto

½ cup walnuts
2 cups watercress plus extra
  sprigs to garnish
1 tablespoon sour cream

- Cook the pasta in a large saucepan of salted boiling water according to the package instructions until al dente.

- Meanwhile, make the watercress pesto. Tip the walnuts into a small skillet and dry-fry over medium heat for 3 minutes, giving the pan a shake every now and again, until they start to turn brown. Allow to cool for a minute or two. Place the nuts, watercress, and sour cream in a small food processor or blender and whiz together to form a pesto. Season well with salt and pepper.

- Drain the pasta, then spoon into serving bowls and arrange slices of the cheese on top. Serve with dollops of the pesto and garnished with watercress sprigs.

 Leek, Onion, and Blue Cheese Spaghetti with Watercress Toss a handful of small shallots and 5 oz baby leeks, trimmed and cleaned, in a little oil. Place on a baking sheet and roast in a preheated oven, 400°F, for 20 minutes or until softened and lightly browned. Meanwhile, cook and drain the spaghetti as above. Stir through the baked shallots and leeks, 5 oz chopped blue cheese, and 2 tablespoons sour cream. Serve topped with a handful of watercress.

Gnocchi with Blue Cheese and Watercress Pesto Make the watercress pesto as above. Cook 8 oz fresh gnocchi according to the package instructions. Drain well and return to the pan. Stir through the watercress pesto, adding an extra 2 tablespoons sour cream, 3 tablespoons milk, and 2 oz chopped blue cheese. Place 1 slice of white bread and a handful of walnuts in a small food processor or blender to form bread crumbs. Spoon the gnocchi into a heatproof dish, sprinkle with the bread crumbs and cook under a preheated medium broiler for 10 minutes or until golden and bubbling.

 # Eggplant and Mozzarella Fusilli Lunghi

Serves 4

4 tablespoons olive oil
1 eggplant, thickly sliced
1¼ cups store-bought tomato pasta sauce
½ teaspoon dried red pepper flakes
14 oz fusilli lunghi
¼ cup grated Parmesan cheese
4 oz mozzarella cheese, cubed
salt and pepper
basil leaves, to garnish

- Heat half the oil in a large nonstick skillet, add half the eggplant, and cook for 5–7 minutes until softened and lightly golden. Season well, then remove from the pan to a plate. Repeat with the remaining oil and eggplant.

- Place the tomato pasta sauce and pepper flakes in a saucepan, add the cooked eggplant and simmer for a couple of minutes.

- Meanwhile, cook the pasta in a large saucepan of salted boiling water according to the package instructions until al dente. Drain, reserving a little of the cooking water, and return to the pan. Stir through the eggplant sauce, adding a little cooking water to loosen if needed.

- Toss through the Parmesan and season, then spoon into serving bowls. Top with the mozzarella and serve sprinkled with the basil.

 ### Simple Eggplant and Mozzarella

Fusilli Cut 7 oz eggplant into thin slices, rub with olive oil, and season well. Cook under a preheated hot broiler for 3–5 minutes on each side. Meanwhile, cook 14 oz fusilli according to the package instructions until al dente. Drain, reserving a little cooking water, and return to the pan. Toss through 5 tablespoons store-bought fresh green pesto, mix in 4 oz cubed mozzarella cheese and the grilled eggplant, adding a little cooking water to loosen if needed. Sprinkle with 3 tablespoons toasted pine nuts.

Fusilli Lunghi with Rich Eggplant Sauce and Mozzarella

Prick 2 eggplants with a fork, place on a baking sheet and bake in a preheated oven, 425°F, for 20 minutes or until soft and lightly charred. Allow to cool for 5 minutes, then peel away the skin. Crush 1 garlic clove in a small bowl and stir together with 3 tablespoons sour cream. Place in a food processor or blender with the eggplant flesh, a squeeze of lemon juice, and a handful of chopped cilantro leaves and whiz together to form a sauce. Meanwhile, cook and drain the fusilli lunghi as above. Stir through the eggplant sauce and serve topped with the mozzarella as above.

Ligurian Potato and Green Bean Pasta with Pesto

Serves 4

10 oz trofie pasta
6 new potatoes, scrubbed
and halved
4 oz green beans, trimmed
salt and pepper

For the pesto

1 cup basil leaves
3 tablespoons toasted pine nuts
plus extra to serve
1 garlic clove, crushed
6 tablespoons extra virgin
olive oil
3 tablespoons grated Parmesan
cheese plus extra to serve

- Cook the pasta in a large saucepan of salted boiling water according to the package instructions until al dente.

- Meanwhile, cook the potatoes in a large saucepan of salted boiling water for 7 minutes. Add the beans and cook for an additional 5 minutes.

- To make the pesto, pound together all the ingredients in a mortar with a pestle to form a chunky pesto and season with salt and pepper. Alternatively, place the ingredients in a small food processor or blender and whiz together.

- Drain the pasta and vegetables and return to a pan. Toss together with the pesto and season.

- Spoon into serving bowls and serve sprinkled with extra Parmesan and toasted pine nuts.

 Quick Bean and Pea Pasta with Red Pesto Cook 1 lb fresh trofie according to the package instructions until al dente. Meanwhile, cook ½ cup frozen fava beans, ½ cup frozen peas and 4 oz trimmed green beans in a separate saucepan of salted boiling water for 3–4 minutes or until tender. Drain the pasta and vegetables and return to a pan. Stir through 4 tablespoons store-bought fresh red pesto and serve immediately.

 Roast Chicken with Potato, Green Bean, and Pesto Pasta Place the potatoes, prepared as above, in a roasting pan and toss in a little olive oil. Place in a preheated oven, 400°C, for 5 minutes. Add 4 boneless chicken breasts to the pan and return to the oven for 20 minutes or until the potatoes and chicken are golden and cooked through. Meanwhile, cook the trofie as above. Add the green beans to the pan 5 minutes before the end of the cooking time and cook until tender. Make the pesto as above and mix together with 2 oz soft goat cheese in a bowl. Drain the pasta and beans and return to the pan. Stir through the pesto and roasted potatoes and serve the pasta alongside the chicken.

Chicken, Bacon, and Asparagus Pasta Bake

Serves 4

2 teaspoons olive oil

2 boneless, skinless chicken breasts

4 Canadian bacon slices

11 oz penne

5 oz asparagus spears, trimmed and thickly sliced

⅔ cup sour cream

6 tablespoons milk

¼ cup grated Parmesan cheese

salt and pepper

- Rub the oil over the chicken breasts and season well with salt and pepper, then cook under a preheated hot broiler for 7 minutes on each side or until golden and cooked through. Add the bacon to the broiler pan when you turn over the chicken and cook until just crisp. Cool slightly, then chop into bite-size pieces.

- Meanwhile, cook the pasta in a large saucepan of salted boiling water according to the package instructions until al dente. Add the asparagus 3 minutes before the end of the cooking time and cook until just tender. Drain well and return to the pan.

- Mix together the sour cream and milk in a bowl, then stir into the pasta. Add the chicken and bacon and season well.

- Spoon into a large heatproof dish and sprinkle the Parmesan on top. Cook under a preheated hot broiler for 5 minutes or until golden and heated through.

10 **Asparagus and Chicken Penne with Prosciutto** Cook the penne as above. Meanwhile, drizzle a little olive oil and balsamic vinegar over 5 oz trimmed asparagus spears. Season, then cook on a hot griddle for 5 minutes, turning frequently, until soft. Chop into pieces. Drain the pasta, reserving a little of the cooking water, and return to the pan. Toss through the asparagus, 1 store-bought roasted chicken breast, skin discarded and torn into strips, and 3 tablespoons sour cream. Serve topped with a slice of prosciutto.

30 **Penne with Poached Chicken and Asparagus** Place 2 boneless, skinless chicken breasts in a saucepan, pour over enough hot chicken stock to cover, and add a good squeeze of lemon juice. Cook over a very gentle heat for 12–15 minutes or until cooked through. Remove from the pan, cut into bite-size pieces, and keep warm. Boil the poaching liquid for 5–10 minutes until reduced, then add 3 tablespoons sour cream and a few finely chopped tarragon leaves. Meanwhile, cook and drain the asparagus and penne as above. Toss through the creamy sauce and chicken. Serve immediately.

PAS-MIDW-BAF

Creamy Anchovy, Lemon, and Arugula Spaghetti

Serves 4

3 oz ciabatta bread
1 tablespoon olive oil
1 garlic clove, crushed
14 oz spaghetti
1¼ cups arugula leaves
salt and pepper

For the anchovy sauce

8 anchovy fillets in oil, drained
3 tablespoons mascarpone
    cheese
juice of ½ lemon
1 egg, lightly beaten
¼ cup grated Parmesan cheese

- Place the ciabatta in a food processor or blender and whiz to form chunky bread crumbs. Heat the oil in a small skillet, add the garlic and stir around the pan, then add the bread crumbs. Cook for 5–7 minutes until golden and crisp all over, then remove from the pan and set aside.

- To make the anchovy sauce, mash the anchovies on a board, using the back of a large knife, to form a paste. Place in a bowl and mix in the mascarpone, then stir in the lemon juice, egg, and Parmesan.

- Cook the pasta in a large saucepan of salted boiling water according to the package instructions until al dente. Drain, reserving a little of the cooking water, and return to the pan. Stir in the anchovy sauce and mix together well, adding a little cooking water to loosen if needed. Season with salt and pepper, then toss through the arugula leaves.

- Spoon into serving bowls and serve sprinkled with the bread crumbs.

10 Spaghetti with Buttery Anchovy, Lemon, and Arugula Sauce

Cook and drain the spaghetti as above. Meanwhile, place 8 drained anchovy fillets in oil, 3½ tablespoons softened butter, the grated zest of 1 lemon and 2 cups arugula leaves in a food processor or blender and whiz together. Stir the butter through the drained pasta and serve immediately.

30 Caramelized Onion, Cavalo Nero, and Anchovy Spaghetti

Heat a little butter and olive oil in a skillet, add 1 sliced onion, and cook over very low heat for 20–25 minutes until caramelized. Meanwhile, heat a little olive oil in a saucepan, add 1 sliced garlic clove, and cook over low heat until softened. Add 5 oz cavalo nero and cook for 1–2 minutes, then pour over 6 tablespoons hot chicken stock and cook for an additional 5 –7 minutes until tender. Make the anchovy sauce and cook and drain the spaghetti as above. Stir the caramelized onion, anchovy sauce, and cavalo nero and any juices through the drained pasta. Serve immediately.

10 Chorizo and Red Pepper Pasta

Serves 2

7 oz fiorelli pasta
1 tablespoon olive oil, plus extra
   to serve
3 fl oz chorizo, thinly sliced
1 red bell pepper, cored, seeded
   and cut into chunks
1 garlic clove, crushed
c tablespoon tomato paste
5 tablespoons dry white wine
1 teaspoon sugar
salt and pepper
chopped flat-leaf parsley,
   to garnish

- Cook the pasta in a large saucepan of salted boiling water according to the package instructions until al dente.

- Meanwhile, heat the oil in a large skillet, add the chorizo slices and cook, for a couple of seconds until crisp. Remove with a slotted spoon and set aside.

- Add the red pepper to the pan and cook for a couple of minutes until browned. Stir in the garlic and tomato paste and cook for an additional 30 seconds. Pour over the wine, add the sugar and stir well. Bring to a boil, then cook for 5 minutes until reduced slightly and season with salt and pepper.

- Drain the pasta and return to the pan. Toss with a little olive oil, then stir through the chorizo and sauce. Spoon into serving bowls and serve sprinkled with the parsley.

---

20 Paella-Style Red Pepper Pasta

Cook 1 boneless chicken breast under a preheated hot broiler for 7 minutes on each side or until cooked through. Meanwhile, heat the olive oil in a large saucepan and fry 4 oz chorizo, cubed, and 1 red bell pepper, prepared as above, until browned, then add the wine as above, a pinch of saffron threads, and 1 lb cleaned clams. Cover with a lid and cook for 5 minutes, shaking occasionally, until the clams open. Discard any that remain closed. Cook 7 oz orzo according to the package instructions. Drain, then toss through the clam sauce and sliced chicken.

30 Pasta with Rich Red Pepper Sauce

Place the red bell pepper, prepared as above, and 3 halved tomatoes in a roasting pan and drizzle with a little olive oil and a splash of white wine. Place in a preheated oven, 375°F, for 20–25 minutes. Meanwhile, cook and drain the fiorelli as above. Sprinkle the pepper and tomatoes with 1 teaspoon smoked paprika, then toss through the drained pasta. Serve with dollops of sour cream.

Linguine with Seafood in a Tomato Sauce

Serves 2

3 tablespoons olive oil

2 garlic cloves, sliced

1 red chili, seeded if desired, and finely chopped

5 tablespoons dry white wine

1¼ cups seeded and chopped tomatoes

1 lb mussels, debearded and cleaned

7 oz linguine

handful of flat-leaf parsley, chopped

salt and pepper

- Heat the oil in a large saucepan, add the garlic and chili and cook for a couple of seconds until beginning to brown. Pour in the wine and cook for a couple of minutes until reduced by half. Stir in the tomatoes and cook for an additional 5 minutes, adding a little water if needed.

- Add the mussels to the pan, cover with a lid, and cook for 5 minutes, shaking occasionally, until the mussels open. Discard any that remain closed.

- Meanwhile, cook the pasta in a large saucepan of salted boiling water according to the package instructions until al dente. Drain, toss through the mussel sauce, and season with salt and pepper. Sprinkle with the parsley and serve immediately.

 Quick Seafood Linguine Cook the linguine as above. Meanwhile, heat 2 tablespoons olive oil in a skillet, add 6 large scallops, and cook for 2 minutes on each side or until just cooked through. Drain the pasta and return to the pan. Stir through the scallops, a good squeeze of lemon juice, 2 seeded and chopped tomatoes, and a pinch of dried red pepper flakes. Serve immediately.

Cajun-Style Seafood Linguine Heat a little olive oil in a skillet, add 5 oz sliced smoked sausage and fry until golden. Add 1 chopped onion and cook until softened. Stir in 2 crushed garlic cloves and 1 teaspoon Cajun seasoning. Pour over a 13 oz can chopped tomatoes and simmer for 20 minutes. Add the mussels, prepared as above, and continue as above.

20 Spaghetti Salsa Verde with Broiled Chicken

Serves 4

1 tablespoon olive oil
2 boneless, skinless chicken
 breasts
14 oz spaghetti
salt and pepper

For the salsa verde

large handful of flat-leaf parsley
small handful of basil leaves
1 garlic clove, crushed
5 tablespoons extra virgin
 olive oil
grated zest of 1 lemon, plus a
 squeeze of lemon juice
1–2 tablespoons capers, rinsed
 and drained

- Rub the 1 tablespoon oil over the chicken breasts and season well. Cook under a preheated hot broiler for 7 minutes on each side or until golden and cooked through.

- Meanwhile, cook the pasta in a large saucepan of salted boiling water according to the package instructions until al dente.

- To make the salsa verde, place the herbs, garlic, oil, lemon zest and lemon juice in a small food processor or blender. Pulse for a couple of seconds, then add the capers and pulse a few more times to form a thick paste.

- Drain the pasta, reserving a little of the cooking water, and return to the pan. Stir through the salsa verde, adding a little cooking water to loosen if needed, and season with salt and pepper.

- Cut the chicken into thick slices. Spoon the pasta onto serving plates and serve topped with the sliced chicken.

---

10 Simple Chicken and Salsa Verde Pasta Salad Cook 1 lb fresh penne according to the package instructions until al dente. Meanwhile, make the salsa verde as above. Drain the pasta, then cool under cold running water and drain again. Tip into a serving dish and stir through the salsa verde. Add 2 store-bought roasted chicken breasts, skin discarded and flesh torn into shreds, and 3 drained and chopped sundried tomatoes in oil.

30 Chicken Pasta Soup with Salsa Verde Place 1 sliced peeled carrot, 3 boneless, skinless chicken thighs, and 6 cups hot chicken stock in a large saucepan and gently poach for 20 minutes or until the chicken is cooked through. Remove the chicken with a slotted spoon and cool slightly, then cut into small strips. Return to the pan with a large handful of chopped Savoy cabbage and cook for 5 minutes until cooked through. Meanwhile, cook 4 oz orzo according to the package instructions. Make the salsa verde as above. Drain the pasta, add to the soup, and heat through. Serve with the salsa verde sauce drizzled over.

1 Fava Bean, Tomato, and Goat Cheese Pasta

Serves 2

7 oz tricolore trottole pasta

½ frozen fava beans, skinned if desired

1 tablespoon olive oil

1 garlic clove, sliced

½ cup cherry tomatoes

2 oz soft goat cheese

salt and pepper

oregano leaves, to garnish

- Cook the pasta in a large saucepan of salted boiling water according to the package instructions until al dente. Add the fava beans 3–4 minutes before the end of the cooking time and cook until tender.

- Meanwhile, heat the oil in a large skillet, add the garlic, and cook for 30 seconds, then stir in the tomatoes. Cook for a couple of minutes until soft, then squash with the back of a spoon to make a very rough sauce. Season well with salt and pepper.

- Drain the pasta, reserving a little of the cooking water, and return to the pan. Toss through the tomato sauce, adding a little cooking water to loosen if needed.

- Spoon into serving bowls and crumble over the goat cheese. Serve sprinkled with the oregano leaves.

---

2 Fava Bean, Tomato, and Pancetta Pasta with Goat Cheese

Heat a little olive oil in a large skillet, add 5 slices of pancetta, cut into thin strips, and cook until turning golden. Add 1 sliced garlic clove and 3 tablespoons dry white wine and cook until reduced, then add 1 cup chopped tomatoes. Cook for 10 minutes, adding a little water. Meanwhile, cook the tricolore trottole and fava beans as above. Drain and stir through the sauce with a handful of chopped oregano leaves. Serve with the goat cheese as above.

3 Tomato and Goat Cheese Open Lasagna with Fava Bean Salad

Make the tomato sauce as above, adding 5 drained and chopped sundried tomatoes in oil with the cherry tomatoes. Pour over 6 tablespoons hot chicken stock and simmer for 10 minutes. Meanwhile, cook 4 dried lasagna sheets in a large saucepan of salted boiling water for 7–10 minutes or until soft, then drain well. Cut the sheets in half and lay one half-sheet on each of 4 plates. Divide half the sauce and 3 oz crumbled soft goat cheese over the pasta, then repeat the layers, finishing with goat cheese. Toss ½ cup cooked and skinned fava beans with a little chopped shallot, 1 cup baby salad leaves, a squeeze of lemon juice, and 2 tablespoons extra virgin olive oil in a bowl. Arrange around each plate and serve immediately.

30 Mexican Chicken Tagliatelle

Serves 4

3 tablespoons olive oil
1 onion, finely chopped
2 garlic cloves, finely chopped
1 tablespoon tomato paste
13 oz can chopped tomatoes
1 teaspoon chipotle paste or
   chipotle sauce
2 boneless, skinless chicken
   breasts
14 oz tagliatelle
3 tablespoons sour cream
salt and pepper
chopped cilantro leaves,
   to garnish

- Heat 2 tablespoons of the oil in a saucepan, add the onion and cook for 3 minutes, stirring often. Add the garlic and cook for 2–3 minutes or until softened. Stir in the tomato paste, tomatoes, and chipotle paste or sauce. Simmer for 20 minutes, adding a little water if needed, then season.

- Meanwhile, rub the remaining oil over the chicken breasts and season well. Heat a griddle pan until smoking, add the chicken, and cook for 7 minutes on each side or until lightly charred and cooked through. Alternatively, cook under a preheated hot broiler.

- Cook the pasta in a large saucepan of salted boiling water according to the package instructions until al dente. Drain, reserving a little cooking water. Stir through the tomato sauce, adding a little cooking water to loosen if needed.

- Cut the chicken into bite-size pieces and stir through the pasta. Spoon into serving bowls, sprinkle with the cilantro and serve with dollops of sour cream.

1 Fiery Chicken Pasta Salad Cook 1 lb fresh penne according to the package instructions until al dente. Drain, then cool under cold running water and drain again. Meanwhile, chop 5 seeded tomatoes, 2 scallions, ½ red chili, seeded if desired, and mix in a bowl with a squeeze of lime juice and a drizzle of extra virgin olive oil. Tip the pasta into a serving dish and mix well with the tomato mixture and 1 store-bought roasted chicken breast, skin discarded and flesh shredded.

2 Tagliatelle with Chicken and Spicy Tomato Sauce Place 2 boneless, skinless chicken breasts in a small pan, pour over enough chicken stock to cover, and cook over very gentle heat for 10–15 minutes or until cooked through. Meanwhile, place 1 cup cherry tomatoes and 1 chopped red chili, seeded if desired, in a broiler pan and toss in a little olive oil. Cook under a preheated hot broiler for 10 minutes or until blackened. Peel away the skin, seeds, and membrane. Place in a small food processor or blender with 5 tablespoons sour cream and a handful of cilantro leaves and whiz together. While the chicken and tomatoes are cooking, cook the tagliatelle as above. Drain, reserving a little of the cooking water, and return to the pan. Stir through the tomato sauce, adding a little cooking water to loosen if needed. Cut the chicken into slices and mix in. Serve sprinkled with extra chopped cilantro, if desired.

PAS-MIDW-DYQ

20 Lemony Conchiglie with Tuna and Capers

Serves 4

14 oz conchiglie
1 small garlic clove, crushed
juice and grated zest of ½ lemon
5 tablespoons extra virgin
  olive oil
7½ oz can tuna in oil, drained
2 tablespoons capers, rinsed and
  drained
large handful of flat-leaf parsley,
  chopped
salt and pepper

- Cook the pasta in a large saucepan of salted boiling water according to the package instructions until al dente.

- Meanwhile, mix together the garlic, lemon juice and zest, and olive oil in a bowl. Using a fork, break the tuna into large chunks and carefully stir into the dressing with the capers.

- Drain the pasta, reserving a little of the cooking water, and return to the pan. Stir through the tuna and dressing, adding a little cooking water to loosen if needed. Season well with salt and pepper, then stir in the parsley and serve immediately.

 Quick Tuna, Caper, and Lemon Pasta

Cook 7 oz orzo according to the package instructions. Meanwhile, whisk together 2 tablespoons extra virgin olive oil and a squeeze of lemon juice, then stir in the tuna and capers as above. Drain the pasta and return to the pan. Stir through the tuna dressing, then toss through 1¾ cups chopped arugula leaves. Serve immediately.

 Fresh Tuna, Caper, and Lemon Conchiglie Season 2 thick tuna steaks, rub all over with olive oil, and place in an ovenproof dish. Place in a preheated oven, 225°F, for 20–25 minutes, depending how rare you like it. Meanwhile, cook and drain the conchiglie above. Cut the fish into large chunks and toss through the pasta with a little chopped red onion, 2 tablespoons rinsed and drained capers, a squeeze of lemon juice, and a handful of chopped flat-leaf parsley. Serve at once.

Creamy Broccoli and Anchovy Orecchiette

Serves 4

2 tablespoons olive oil
1 tablespoon butter
1 onion, sliced
3 garlic cloves, sliced
½ teaspoon dried red
   pepper flakes
8 anchovy fillets in oil, drained
6 tablespoons heavy cream
4 oz tenderstem broccoli
14 oz orecchiette pasta
salt and pepper

· Heat the oil and butter in a large skillet, add the onion, and cook for 10 minutes until soft and golden. Add the garlic, pepper flakes, and anchovies and cook for an additional 2–3 minutes or until the anchovies begin to disintegrate. Mash them with the back of a spoon, pour over the cream, and season with salt and pepper.

· Meanwhile, cook the broccoli in a large saucepan of salted boiling water for 3 minutes, then remove with a slotted spoon. Add the pasta to the pan of boiling water and cook according to the package instructions until al dente.

· Stir the broccoli into the anchovy sauce, cover with a lid, and cook for 3–5 minutes or until the broccoli is heated and cooked through.

· Drain the pasta, reserving a little of the cooking water, and stir through the broccoli sauce, adding a little cooking water to loosen if needed. Serve immediately.

 Orecchiette with Chunky Broccoli Sauce Cook 1 lb fresh orecchiette according to the package instructions until al dente. Meanwhile, cook 5 oz purple sprouting broccoli spears in a saucepan of boiling water for 5 minutes until tender. Drain the broccoli and place in a food processor or blender with 1 crushed garlic clove, 3 drained and mashed anchovy fillets in oil, the grated zest and juice of ½ lemon, ¼ cup grated Parmesan cheese, a pinch of dried red pepper flakes, and 4 tablespoons extra virgin olive oil and whiz together to form a chunky sauce. Drain the pasta, reserving a little of the cooking water, and return to the pan. Toss through the broccoli sauce, adding a little cooking water to loosen if needed, and serve immediately.

3 Anchovy Orecchiette with Roasted Broccoli Toss 1 head of broccoli, cut into florets, in 3 tablespoons olive oil and season. Place in an ovenproof dish and bake in a preheated oven, 400°F, for 20–25 minutes until tender and lightly charred. Meanwhile, cook and drain the orecchiette as above. Mash the anchovies as above and 1 garlic clove together in a bowl. Stir through the paste, adding a little cooking water to loosen. Add the roasted broccoli and serve with grated Parmesan cheese.

Chicken Fusilli with Red Pepper and Almond Pesto

Serves 4

14 oz fusilli
2 store-bought roasted chicken
  breasts, about 5 oz each
salt

For the pesto

5 tablespoons extra virgin
  olive oil
2 red bell peppers
large handful of basil leaves,
  plus extra to garnish
3 tablespoons toasted almonds
¼ cup grated Pecorino cheese
  plus extra to serve

- To make the pesto, rub about 1 tablespoon of the olive oil over the red peppers. Cook under a preheated hot broiler for 10 minutes, turning, until charred all over. Put in a plastic food bag, seal, and leave for 5 minutes. When cooled, peel off the blackened skin. Cut in half and remove the seeds.

- Place the roasted peppers in a food processor or blender with the remaining olive oil, basil, almonds, and Pecorino and whiz to form a thick but smooth paste. Add a little more oil or a drizzle of water if needed. Season well with salt.

- Meanwhile, cook the pasta in a large saucepan of salted boiling water according to the package instructions until al dente. Drain, reserving a little of the cooking water, and return to the pan. Stir in the pesto, adding a little cooking water to loosen until the pasta is coated.

- Tear the chicken into strips, discarding the skin, and stir through the pasta. Serve in bowls sprinkled with a little extra chopped basil and grated Pecorino.

10 Easy Red Pepper and Almond Pasta Salad

Cook the fusilli as above. Drain, then cool under cold running water and drain again. Meanwhile, place 3 tablespoons toasted almonds and 4 tablespoons each Pecorino cheese and mayonnaise in a small food processor or blender and whiz together. Tip the pasta into a large dish and toss through the sauce, 2 drained and chopped roasted red peppers from a jar, and a handful of chopped basil leaves. Sprinkle with ¼ cup slivered almonds.

30 Broiled Chicken with Spicy Red Pepper and Almond Fusilli

Rub a little olive oil over 1 red chili and grill alongside the red peppers as above, then make the red pepper and almond pesto as above, adding the peeled and seeded chili. Mix together 3 oz soft goat cheese with a handful of chopped basil leaves in a bowl. Spread a little of the mixture under the skin of 4 boneless chicken breasts, then cook under a preheated hot broiler for about 7 minutes on each side or until cooked through. Meanwhile, cook and drain 10 oz fusilli as above. Stir through the pesto, adding a little cooking water to loosen, and serve alongside the chicken with extra toasted almonds sprinkled over.

Creamy Gorgonzola Gnocchi

Serves 4

2 tablespoons butter
2 leeks, trimmed, cleaned, and sliced
1 onion, sliced
1 garlic clove, finely chopped
5 tablespoons heavy cream
3 oz Gorgonzola cheese
1 lb fresh gnocchi
¼ cup toasted walnuts, roughly chopped
salt and pepper

- Heat the butter in a saucepan, add the leeks and onion and a splash of water and cook over low heat for 15 minutes until very soft. Stir in the garlic and cook for 1 minute more. Add the cream and crumble over the Gorgonzola, then cook until the cheese melts.

- Meanwhile, cook the pasta in a large saucepan of salted boiling water according to the package instructions. Drain, reserving a little of the cooking water, and return to the pan. Stir through the sauce, adding a little cooking water to loosen if needed. Season well with salt and pepper.

- Spoon into serving bowls and serve topped with the walnuts.

10 **Quick Gorgonzola and Spinach Gnocchi**
Cook and drain the gnocchi as above, adding 5 cups baby spinach leaves to the pan before draining. Stir through 3 oz crumbled Gorgonzola cheese and enough cooking water to make a sauce. Serve at once.

 Gnocchi with Roasted Shallots and Gorgonzola Toss 5 oz shallots in 3 tablespoons olive oil and 1 tablespoon balsamic vinegar in a roasting pan, then sprinkle with a few thyme sprigs. Place in a preheated oven, 350°F, for 20–25 minutes until soft and golden. Cook and drain the gnocchi as above. Stir through the roasted shallots, adding a little cooking water to loosen. Serve sprinkled with 3 oz crumbled Gorgonzola cheese.

20 Linguine with Endive, Pancetta, and Mascarpone

Serves 2

1 tablespoon olive oil
2 oz cubed pancetta
1 small onion, sliced
1 garlic clove, sliced
2 red Belgian endive, trimmed
   and thinly sliced
3 tablespoons dry white wine
3 tablespoons hot chicken stock
7 oz linguine
2 tablespoons mascarpone
   cheese
2 tablespoons grated Parmesan
   cheese plus extra to serve
salt and pepper

- Heat the oil in a skillet, add the pancetta and cook, until it begins to brown. Add the onion and cook for 5 minutes or until it begins to soften and turn golden.

- Add the garlic and cook for 30 seconds, then stir in the endive. Cook for a few minutes until it wilts, then pour over the wine. Cook until reduced by half, then pour over the stock and simmer for 7 minutes.

- Meanwhile, cook the pasta in a large saucepan of salted boiling water according to the package instructions until al dente. Drain, reserving a little of the cooking water, and return to the pan.

- Stir the mascarpone and Parmesan into the sauce, season well with salt and pepper, and toss through the pasta, adding a little cooking water to loosen if needed. Spoon onto serving plates and serve sprinkled with extra Parmesan.

 Linguine with Broiled Endive, Pancetta, and Mascarpone

Cook the linguine as above. Toss 2 heads of quartered Belgian endive in a little olive oil. Place on a broiler rack and cook under a hot broiler for 2 minutes on each side, then drizzle with 2 teaspoons balsamic vinegar. Heat a little olive oil in a skillet, add 3 oz pancetta cubes and fry for 5 minutes until golden. Drain the pasta. Return to the pan. Toss through the endive and pancetta. Serve with dollops of mascarpone and grated Parmesan cheese.

 Roasted Endive, Pancetta, and Mascarpone Linguine Halve 4 heads of Belgian endive and place in a roasting pan. Dab with a little butter and then pour over 6 tablespoons chicken stock. Place in a preheated oven, 350°F, for 20–25 minutes or until golden and soft. Meanwhile, cook and drain the linguine and fry the pancetta, onion, and garlic as above. Cut the roasted endive into thin wedges and stir through the pasta with the pancetta mixture, mascarpone, and Parmesan as above.

Shrimp, Tomato, and Feta Rigatoni

Serves 4

2 tablespoons olive oil
1 onion, finely chopped
2 garlic cloves, finely chopped
1 teaspoon tomato paste
juice of ½ lemon
1 teaspoon sugar
½ teaspoon dried red pepper
flakes
13 oz can chopped tomatoes
7 oz frozen large raw peeled
shrimp
14 oz rigatoni
2 oz feta cheese
salt and pepper
chopped flat-leaf parsley,
to garnish

- Heat the oil in a saucepan, add the onion and garlic and cook for a couple of minutes until softened. Stir in the tomato paste, then add the lemon juice, sugar, pepper flakes, and tomatoes. Bring to a boil, then reduce the heat and simmer for 10 minutes.

- Remove the pan from the heat then, using an immersion blender, whiz to a smooth paste. Return to the heat, add the shrimp, and cook for 3–5 minutes or until they have turned pink and are just cooked through and season well.

- Meanwhile, cook the pasta in a large saucepan of salted boiling water according to the package instructions until al dente. Drain, reserving a little of the cooking water, and return to the pan. Stir through the shrimp sauce, adding a little cooking water if needed. Spoon into serving bowls, then crumble over the feta and serve sprinkled with the parsley.

 Shrimp Penne with No-Cook Tomato Sauce and Feta Cook 1 lb fresh penne according to package instructions until al dente. Add the shrimp to the pan 5 minutes before the end of the cooking time and cook until they are pink and are cooked through. Meanwhile, mix 2 chopped and seeded tomatoes, 1 tablespoon sweet chili sauce, and a handful of chopped basil leaves in a bowl. Drain the pasta and shrimp and return to the pan. Drizzle with olive oil, mix in the tomato sauce, and serve with 2 oz feta cheese.

One-Pot Tomato, Shrimp, and Feta Rigatoni Heat 1 lb store-bought tomato sauce with ¾ cup fish stock. Simmer for 10 minutes, as above, then stir 14 oz rigatoni into the pan and cook for an additional 10 minutes, stirring occasionally. Stir through the shrimp as above and cook for 3–5 minutes or until they have turned pink and are just cooked through. Mix together 2 oz crumbled feta cheese, a handful of fresh white bread crumbs, and a handful of chopped flat-leaf parsley and sprinkle over. Cook under a preheated hot broiler for a couple of minutes until golden.

Bucatini with Sardines and Fennel

Serves 4

pinch of saffron threads
5 tablespoons boiling water
3 tablespoons olive oil
1 garlic clove, finely chopped
1 cup fresh white bread crumbs
14 oz bucatini pasta
1 onion, chopped
1 fennel bulb, chopped
1 teaspoon fennel seeds
2 anchovy fillets in oil, drained
2 tablespoons raisins
4 sardines, boned and filleted
2 tablespoons toasted pine nuts
handful of dill weed, chopped
salt and pepper

- Place the saffron in a small bowl and pour over the measurement water. Allow to stand for 5 minutes. Meanwhile, heat 1 tablespoon of the oil in a small skillet, add the garlic and bread crumbs, and cook for a couple of minutes until golden. Set aside.

- Cook the pasta in a large saucepan of salted boiling water according to the pack instructions until al dente. Meanwhile, heat another tablespoon of the oil in a large skillet, add the onion and both kinds of fennel, and cook for 5 minutes to soften. Mash in the anchovies, then add the saffron with its soaking water. Add the raisins and let it bubble for 2 minutes.

- Rub the remaining tablespoon of oil over the sardine fillets and season well. Cook on a preheated hot griddle pan or under a hot broiler for 3 minutes on each side or until cooked through. Drain the pasta, reserving a little of the cooking water, and return to the pan. Toss through the sauce, adding a little cooking water to loosen if needed. Season well. Spoon onto serving plates, top with the sardine fillets. Serve sprinkled with the pine nuts, bread crumbs, and dill.

 Quick Sardine Spaghettini

Cook 14 oz spaghettini according to the package instructions until al dente. Meanwhile, place a 4 oz can sardines in tomato sauce and 1 chopped tomato in a small saucepan and heat through. Stir in 1 tablespoon rinsed and drained capers. Drain the pasta, reserving some cooking water, and return to the pan. Stir through the sauce, adding a little cooking water to loosen, and serve immediately.

Sardine and Tomato Bucatini with Walnut Pesto Heat a little olive oil in a saucepan, add 1 chopped tomato, and gently cook until softened. Add 1 chopped garlic clove and a splash of balsamic vinegar, then pour over 1¼ cups pureed tomato and cook for 10 minutes. Add a drained 4 oz can sardines in oil and cook for an additional 10 minutes. Meanwhile, cook and drain the bucatini as above. Place ¾ cup walnuts, 1 garlic clove, a squeeze of lemon juice, 1 tablespoon rinsed and drained capers, 5 tablespoons extra virgin olive oil, and a handful of basil leaves in a food processor or blender and whiz together to form a pesto. Stir the sardine sauce through the drained pasta and serve with the walnut pesto drizzled over.

Tortelloni with Easy Olive and Tomato Sauce

Serves 4

2 tablespoons olive oil
1 garlic clove, sliced
½ cup pitted black olives
10 halved cherry tomatoes
handful of basil leaves
1 lb cheese tortelloni
salt and pepper

- Heat a medium skillet until hot, then add the oil. Add the garlic and olives and cook for 30 seconds until beginning to sizzle, then tip in the tomatoes and cook for a couple of minutes or until the tomatoes are beginning to soften. Season with salt and pepper and stir in the basil leaves.

- Meanwhile, cook the pasta in a large saucepan of salted boiling water according to the package instructions. Drain and toss together with the tomato sauce. Serve immediately.

 Farfalle with Olive Tapenade and Tomato Cook 14 oz farfalle according to the package instructions until al dente. Meanwhile, place 1 crushed garlic clove, the juice of ½ lemon, 3 drained anchovy fillets in oil, ⅔ cup pitted black olives, a handful of flat-leaf parsley, and 3 tablespoons extra virgin olive oil in a food processor or blender and whiz together to form a rough paste. Drain the pasta, reserving a little of the cooking water, and return to the pan. Stir through the tapenade, adding a little cooking water to loosen, and 2 chopped tomatoes. Serve immediately.

Homemade Four-Cheese Pasta Pockets with Tomato and Olive Sauce Mix together 6 tablespoons cream cheese, 3 oz dolcelatte cheese, ¾ cup grated Gruyère cheese and ¼ cup grated Parmesan cheese, in a bowl. Lay 4 store-bought fresh pasta sheets on a lightly floured work surface. Using a 4 inch cutter, stamp out 16 rounds from the sheets. Alternatively, use 16 wonton or gyoza wrappers. Brush a little egg yolk around the edges of the rounds and place 1 teaspoon of the filling in the center of each, then fold in half and use your fingers to seal. Cook in batches in a large saucepan of salted boiling water for 3 minutes. Meanwhile, heat through 1½ cups store-bought tomato pasta sauce and ½ cup pitted black olives in a saucepan. Drain the pasta and return to the pan, then toss through the tomato sauce. Serve immediately.

Spanish Seafood Pasta

Serves 4

2 tablespoons olive oil
1 onion, finely chopped
1 garlic clove, crushed
1 teaspoon tomato paste
1 teaspoon paprika
½ cup dry white wine
13 oz can chopped tomatoes
4 cups hot chicken stock
10 oz angel hair pasta
7 oz mussels, debearded and
  cleaned
4 oz large cooked unpeeled
  shrimp
3 oz prepared squid rings, cleaned

- Heat the oil in a large saucepan, add the onion and garlic, and cook over medium heat for 5 minutes or until softened. Stir in the tomato paste and paprika, then pour over the wine and bubble for 1–2 minutes until reduced a little. Pour in the tomatoes and stock and bring to a boil.

- Break the pasta into small lengths about 1 inch long. Reduce the heat so the mixture is simmering and stir the pasta into the pan. Cover with a lid and cook for 7 minutes, stirring occasionally to stop the pasta from sticking.

- Add the mussels, cover, and cook for 3 minutes until the mussels begin to open. Add the squid rings and shrimp and cook for an additional 2 minutes or until the seafood is cooked through and all the mussels have opened. Discard any mussels that remain closed.

- Bring the pan to the table and serve.

1 **Seafood Pasta Salad** Cook 10 oz orzo according to the package instructions. Add 4 oz cooked peeled shrimp 3 minutes and 3 oz squid rings 1 minute before the end of the cooking time and cook until the seafood is cooked through. Cool under cold water and drain again. Tip into a serving dish and toss with a squeeze of lemon juice, 2 tablespoons extra virgin olive oil, 2 chopped tomatoes, 1¼ cups arugula leaves, and a handful of pitted black olives.

3 **Spanish Seafood Pasta with Chicken** Rub a little olive oil over 2 boneless chicken breasts and place in a roasting pan. Cook in a preheated oven, 400°F, for 20 minutes or until cooked through. Meanwhile, make the recipe as above. Cut the chicken into slices, discarding the skin, and add to the pan with the squid for the last 2 minutes of cooking.

 # Linguine with Spicy Lamb Sauce

Serves 4

2 tablespoons olive oil
4 lamb chops, boned
14 oz linguine
2 garlic cloves, sliced
1 red chili, seeded if desired,
   and sliced
3 tablespoons dry white wine
salt and pepper
chopped mint leaves, to garnish

- Brush a little of the oil over the lamb chops, season well with salt and pepper, and cook under a preheated hot broiler for 5–7 minutes on each side or until golden and just cooked through. Trim away the fat and cut into thin slices.

- Meanwhile, cook the pasta in a large saucepan of salted boiling water according to the package instructions until al dente.

- Heat a saucepan and add the remaining oil. Add the garlic and chili and gently fry for 1 minute until the garlic is golden, then pour over the wine and cook until reduced by half. Season well.

- Drain the pasta and return to the pan, then toss through the sauce and lamb slices and season. Spoon into serving bowls and serve sprinkled with the mint.

 ### Linguine with Stir-Fried Lamb

Cook the linguine as above. Meanwhile, cut 2 lamb chops into thin strips. Heat 2 tablespoons olive oil in a wok or large skillet, add the lamb strips and 2 sliced garlic cloves and stir-fry for 5 minutes or until just cooked through. Add ½ cup pitted black olives 1 minute before the end of the cooking time. Squeeze over the juice of 1 lemon and stir in a handful of chopped mint leaves. Drain the pasta and return to the pan. Toss through the lamb and olives and serve immediately.

Linguine with Lamb, Zucchini, and Tomato Sauce

Heat a little olive oil in a skillet, add 2 sliced garlic cloves and cook for 30 seconds. Add 3 drained and chopped sundried tomatoes in oil, 4 chopped fresh tomatoes, a splash of dry white wine, and 6 tablespoons water. Cook for 20 minutes until the sauce has thickened. Broil and slice the lamb as above. Rub oil over 2 thickly sliced zucchini and cook under the broiler for 5 minutes, turning once. While the lamb is broiling, cook and drain the linguine as above. Stir the broiled zucchini and lamb into the tomato sauce and heat through, then stir the sauce through the drained pasta. Serve with goat cheese crumbled over.

 # Sweet Potato and Spinach Penne

Serves 4

2 sweet potatoes, peeled and cut into bite-size pieces
1 head of garlic, cloves separated
4 tablespoons olive oil
1 tablespoon white balsamic vinegar
14 oz penne
5 cups baby spinach leaves
2 oz feta cheese
salt and pepper

- Place the sweet potato and garlic on a baking sheet. Drizzle over 2 tablespoons of the oil and toss until coated, then season with salt and pepper. Place in a preheated oven, 350°F, for 15–20 minutes until the sweet potato is soft and lightly charred.

- Squeeze the garlic out of its skin into a bowl and mash lightly with a fork to form a paste, then stir in the vinegar and remaining oil. Season well.

- Meanwhile, cook the pasta in a large saucepan of salted boiling water according to the package instructions until al dente. Tip in the spinach, then drain and return to the pan.

- Stir the garlic sauce into the pasta with the roasted sweet potato. Spoon onto serving plates and serve with the feta cheese crumbled over.

 Quick Sweet Potato and Spinach Penne

Cook the penne as above. Add 2 peeled sweet potatoes, cut into bite-size pieces, to the pan 7 minutes before the end of the cooking time and cook until soft. Add 5 cups baby spinach leaves, then drain and return to the pan. Toss together with 6 oz tablespoons ricotta cheese mixed with ¼ cups grated Parmesan cheese. Serve immediately.

 Penne with Spinach and Sweet Potato Sauce Halve 2 sweet potatoes and place on a baking sheet. Roast in a preheated oven, 350°F, for 25–30 minutes until softened. Scoop out the flesh with a fork and mash together with ⅓ cup mascarpone cheese in a bowl. Meanwhile, cook the penne and spinach as above. Drain, reserving a little of the cooking water, and return to the pan. Toss through the sweet potato sauce, adding a little cooking water to loosen. Serve immediately.

Pasta with Pork and Mushrooms in a White Wine Sauce

Serves 4

2 tablespoons olive oil
1 onion, finely chopped
1 garlic clove, finely chopped
14½ oz ground pork
1 tablespoon tomato paste
1 cup dry white wine
⅔ cup hot chicken stock
5 oz mushrooms, trimmed and chopped
5 tablespoons heavy cream
14 oz lumaconi pasta
¼ cup grated Parmesan cheese plus extra to serve
salt and pepper
chopped flat-leaf parsley, to garnish

- Heat 1 tablespoon of the oil in a large skillet, add the onion, and cook for a couple of minutes until beginning to soften. Add the garlic and pork and cook, breaking up the meat with the back of a spoon, for 5–10 minutes or until the meat is golden.

- Stir in the tomato paste and cook for 1 minute more. Pour over the wine and cook until reduced by half, then add the chicken stock and simmer for 10 minutes.

- Heat the remaining oil in a separate skillet. Add the mushrooms and cook for 3 minutes or until golden and soft. Add to the pork, then stir in the cream.

- Meanwhile, cook the pasta in a large saucepan of salted boiling water according to the package instructions until al dente. Drain, reserving a little of the cooking water, and return to the pan. Stir through the sauce and Parmesan, adding a little cooking water to loosen if needed. Season well with salt and pepper.

- Spoon into serving bowls and serve sprinkled with the parsley and extra Parmesan.

Mushroom and Prosciutto Pasta

Cook and drain 14 oz penne. Meanwhile, fry the mushrooms as above, adding 1 chopped garlic clove. When golden, stir through the pasta with the grated zest and juice of 1 lemon and 6 slices of prosciutto, torn into strips. Toss through a handful of arugula leaves, if desired. Serve immediately.

Pasta with Spicy Pork and Mushrooms

Cook 4 thin pork chops under a preheated medium broiler for 7 minutes on each side or until cooked through. Add the mushrooms to the broiler pan 5 minutes before the end of the cooking time. Mix together the grated zest and juice of 1 lemon, 1 teaspoon fennel seeds, 1 chopped red chili, seeded if desired, and 5 tablespoons sour cream in a bowl. Meanwhile, cook and drain the lumaconi as above. Slice the pork into thin strips and toss through the pasta with the mushrooms, sour cream, and 2 chopped tomatoes. Serve immediately.

QuickCook
Family Favorites

Recipes listed by cooking time

30

20

30 Cheesy Tomato Pasta Bake

Serves 4

2 tablespoons olive oil, plus extra
   for greasing
2 garlic cloves, finely chopped
13 oz can chopped tomatoes
handful of oregano leaves,
   chopped, plus extra to garnish
14 oz penne
8 oz mozzarella cheese, cubed
½ cup grated Parmesan cheese
salt and pepper

- Heat the oil in a large skillet, add the garlic, and cook for 30 seconds. Stir in the tomatoes and oregano and simmer, fairly vigorously, for 10–12 minutes or until thickened. Season well with salt and pepper.

- Meanwhile, cook the pasta in a large saucepan of salted boiling water according to the package instructions until al dente. Drain, reserving a little of the cooking water, and return to the pan. Stir in the tomato sauce, reserving 2 tablespoons of the sauce. Add a little cooking water to loosen if needed.

- Spoon half the pasta into a greased ovenproof dish. Cover with half the mozzarella and Parmesan, then add the remaining pasta. Spoon over the reserved tomato sauce and sprinkle with the remaining cheese.

- Place in a preheated oven, 400°F, for 15 minutes or until golden and bubbling and serve.

 Simple Cheese and Tomato Penne

Cook and drain the penne as above. Stir through 4 chopped tomatoes, 3 tablespoons sour cream, and a handful of chopped arugula leaves. Served topped with 5 oz sliced mozzarella cheese and a little grated Parmesan cheese.

 Bubbling Tomato, Cheese, and Ham

Penne Cook the penne as above. Meanwhile, place 2 cups store-bought tomato pasta sauce and 7 oz ham, cut into chunks, in a large saucepan and heat through. Drain the pasta and stir through the sauce. Spoon into a heatproof dish, then sprinkle with 1½ cups grated Gruyère cheese and cook under a preheated medium broiler for 10 minutes or until golden and bubbling.

Four-Cheese Pasta with Watercress Salad

Serves 4

14 oz messicani pasta
¾ cup mascarpone cheese or
cream cheese
3 oz mild Gorgonzola cheese,
crumbled
¾ cup grated Fontina cheese
¼ cup grated Parmesan cheese
salt and pepper

For the watercress salad

1 teaspoon white wine vinegar
1 tablespoon extra virgin olive oil
2 cups watercress

- Cook the pasta in a large saucepan of salted boiling water according to the package instructions until al dente. Drain, reserving at least 3 tablespoons of the cooking water, and return to the pan. Stir in the cheeses, adding enough of the cooking water to make a creamy sauce, and season with salt and pepper.

- Whisk together the vinegar and oil, then toss together with the watercress in a bowl and season well.

- Spoon the pasta into serving bowls and serve topped with the watercress salad.

---

10 Four-Cheese Tortelloni with Yogurt and Watercress

Tip ⅔ cup natural yogurt into a heatproof bowl, place over a saucepan of simmering water (making sure the bottom of the bowl doesn't touch the water), and heat through for 5 minutes. Meanwhile, cook 1 lb four-cheese tortelloni according to the package instructions, then drain and return to the pan. Toss through the yogurt and a handful of chopped watercress. Serve immediately.

30 Four-Cheese Penne and Watercress Bake Cook 14 oz penne according to the package instructions until al dente. Meanwhile, cook 6 bacon slices under a preheated medium broiler for 10 minutes or until crisp. Cool for 1 minute, then cut into bite-size pieces. Mix together the four cheeses as above with 6 tablespoons milk in a bowl. Drain the pasta and return to the pan. Stir through the bacon and cheese sauce, add 2½ cups watercress, chopped

then place in a heatproof dish. Top with 1 cup fresh white bread crumbs and cook under a preheated medium broiler for 15 minutes or until golden and bubbling.

No-Chop Tomato and Arugula Pasta Salad

Serves 4

11 oz tricolore trofie
3 tablespoons mayonnaise
3 tablespoons plain yogurt
¼ cup grated Parmesan cheese
½ cup sunblush tomatoes in oil, drained
2 cups arugula leaves
salt and pepper

- Cook the pasta in a large saucepan of salted boiling water according to the package instructions until al dente. Drain, then cool under cold running water and drain again.

- Meanwhile, mix together the mayonnaise, yogurt, and Parmesan in a large serving bowl and season with salt and pepper. Stir the tomatoes and arugula through the pasta and serve the mayonnaise alongside the pasta.

 Tomato and Arugula Orzo Cook and drain 11 oz orzo according to the package instructions. Meanwhile, place ½ cup drained sunblush tomatoes in oil and 3 tablespoons plain yogurt in a food processor or blender and whiz to form a sauce. Toss through the drained pasta with 2 cups arugula leaves. Serve immediately.

 Eggplant, Tomato, and Arugula Warm Pasta Salad Cut 1 eggplant into cubes and place in an ovenproof dish. Toss with plenty of olive oil and sprinkle with salt and a little dried chili. Cook in a preheated oven, 350°F, for 20–25 minutes or until soft. Allow to cool slightly. Meanwhile, cook the pasta as above. Drain and cool a little, then tip into a serving dish. Toss with 1 tablespoon balsamic vinegar, the sunblush tomatoes as above, the eggplant, and 2 tablespoons extra virgin olive oil. Toss through the arugula to serve.

 # Pea Fusilli with Bacon and Ricotta

Serves 4

5 tablespoons olive oil
2 garlic cloves
1¼ cups frozen peas
handful of mint leaves, chopped,
plus extra to garnish (optional)
squeeze of lemon juice, plus
grated lemon zest to garnish
14 oz fusilli
4 bacon slices
¼ cup grated Parmesan cheese,
plus extra to serve
½ cup ricotta cheese, crumbled
salt and pepper

- Heat the oil in a small skillet, add the garlic, and cook over a very low heat for 5 minutes or until soft and golden.

- Cook the peas in a small saucepan of boiling water for 2–3 minutes or until just tender. Drain, then cool under cold running water and drain again. Place half the peas, the garlicky oil, reserving a little to coat the pasta, the garlic cloves, mint, lemon juice to taste, and salt and pepper in a food processor or blender and whiz together.

- Cook the pasta in a large saucepan of salted boiling water according to the package instructions until al dente. Cook the bacon under a preheated medium broiler for 10 minutes, turning once, or until crisp and cooked through.

- Drain the pasta, reserving a little of the cooking water, and return to the pan. Toss through the reserved garlicky oil, adding a little cooking water to loosen. Stir through the whole peas and Parmesan, spoon into serving bowls, top with dollops of the pea puree, the ricotta, crumble over the bacon, and serve with extra mint leaves and Parmesan.

 Melting Pea and Pesto Fusilli with Bacon and Ricotta Cook the fusilli as above. Add the peas to the pan 2–3 minutes before the end of the cooking time and cook until tender. Meanwhile, cook the bacon as above. Drain the pasta and peas, return to the pan and stir through 5 tablespoons store-bought green pesto. Cut 4 oz mozzarella into chunks and stir in the pasta until starting to melt. Serve, sprinkled with the bacon and ricotta as above.

Pea, Bacon, and Ricotta Pasta Bakes Cook 11 oz angel hair pasta according to the package instructions. Add the peas to the pan 2–3 minutes before the end of the cooking time and cook until just tender. Drain, then cool under cold running water and drain again. Mix together 1 cup ricotta, 5 beaten eggs, 3 crumbled broiled bacon slices, the grated zest of 1 lemon, and a handful of chopped basil leaves in a large bowl, then stir in the pasta and peas. Grease 12 cups of a muffin pan, then divide the mixture between the cups. Top with ¼ cup grated cheddar cheese and place in a preheated oven, 400°F, for 15 minutes or until golden and cooked through.

Tomato Soup with Pasta Shapes

Serves 4

2 tablespoons olive oil
1 onion, finely chopped
1 carrot, peeled and finely
  chopped
1 celery stick, finely chopped
2 teaspoons tomato paste
13 oz can chopped tomatoes
1 teaspoon sugar
1 cup hot vegetable stock
handful of basil leaves, chopped
4 oz alphabet pasta
salt

- Heat the oil in a large saucepan, add the vegetables, and cook for 5 minutes until softened. Add the tomato paste, tomatoes, sugar, and stock and bring to a boil. Reduce the heat, then simmer for 12 minutes.

- Stir in the basil, then remove the pan from the heat. Using an immersion blender, whiz together to form a smooth soup.

- Meanwhile, cook the pasta in a large saucepan of salted boiling water for 2 minutes less than directed on the package instructions. Drain, then stir into the soup and return to the heat.

- Simmer for another couple of minutes or until the pasta is cooked through. Ladle into serving bowls.

 Quick Arugula and Tomato Pasta Shapes Heat a little olive oil in a large saucepan, add 1 chopped garlic clove, and gently cook until softened. Add 4 oz alphabet or stelline pasta, then stir in ⅔ cup hot vegetable stock and 2 chopped tomatoes. Bring to a boil, then cover with a lid and simmer for 5 minutes or until the pasta is cooked through and the liquid has been absorbed. Toss through a handful of arugula leaves, then serve immediately.

 Fresh Tomato Soup with Pasta Shapes Place 2 lb tomatoes in a heatproof bowl and pour over boiling water to cover. Leave for 1–2 minutes, then drain, cut a cross at the stem end of each tomato, and peel off the skins. Halve the tomatoes, remove the seeds, and roughly chop. Make the tomato soup as above, replacing the canned tomatoes with the fresh tomatoes and adding a little more stock to the soup if needed.

3 Ham and Zucchini Lasagna

Serves 4

2 cups store-bought tomato
pasta sauce
6 slices of ham, cut into bite-size
pieces
handful of basil leaves, chopped
1 zucchini, grated
8 fresh lasagna sheets
⅔ cup sour cream
6 tablespoons water
¼ cup grated Parmesan cheese
salt and pepper

- Place the tomato pasta sauce in a saucepan and heat through, then stir in the ham, basil, and zucchini and season with salt and pepper.

- Meanwhile, prepare the lasagna sheets, if necessary, according to the package instructions. Mix together the sour cream and measurement water in a bowl until smooth.

- Spread a third of the tomato sauce over the bottom of a medium ovenproof dish. Drizzle a quarter of the sour cream over the sauce, then top with a third of the lasagna sheets, cutting to fit the dish, if necessary. Repeat with the remaining ingredients, finishing with the remaining sour cream, and sprinkle with the Parmesan.

- Place in a preheated oven, 400°F, for 15 minutes or until bubbling and cooked through.

 Prosciutto and Zucchini Open Lasagna Cook 8 fresh lasagna sheets in a large saucepan of salted boiling water for 3–5 minutes or until soft, then drain well and cut into squares. Meanwhile, heat the zucchini and basil in the tomato pasta sauce as above, adding 4 slices of chopped prosciutto. Pile up the lasagna squares on a plate, layering with the tomato sauce. Serve topped with a dollop of sour cream.

 Bacon and Zucchini Linguine Cook 14 oz linguine according to the package instructions until al dente. Meanwhile, cut 2 zucchini into thick slices. Cook under a preheated medium broiler with 6 bacon slices for 5–10 minutes, turning once, until golden and cooked through. Place 3 tablespoons heavy cream and the grated zest of 1 lemon in a small saucepan and cook until reduced a little. Drain the pasta and return to the pan. Chop the bacon slices, then stir through the pasta with the cream, broiled zucchini, and bacon and a handful of arugula leaves. Serve immediately.

Chicken Fettuccine Alfredo

Serves 4

2 boneless, skinless chicken
  breasts
14 oz fettuccine
2 tablespoons butter
½ cup light cream
½ cup grated Parmesan cheese
salt and pepper
finely sliced chives, to garnish

- Place the chicken breasts in a small pan, pour over enough water to cover and simmer for 12–15 minutes or until just cooked through.

- Meanwhile, cook the pasta in a large saucepan of salted boiling water according to the package instructions until al dente.

- Melt the butter in a separate saucepan, then stir in the cream and simmer for 1–2 minutes and season well with salt and pepper. Using a fork, break the chicken into bite-size pieces.

- Drain the pasta, reserving a little of the cooking water, and return to the pan. Toss through the chicken, creamy sauce, and Parmesan, adding a little cooking water to loosen if needed. Season well.

- Spoon into serving bowls and serve sprinkled with the chives.

Quick Chicken Spaghetti Alfredo

Cook 14 oz quick-cook spaghetti and the cream sauce as above. Drain the pasta, reserving a little of the cooking water, and return to the pan. Toss through 2 store-bought roasted chicken breasts, skin discarded and torn into shreds, the sauce, and Parmesan as above. Serve immediately.

Chicken Fettuccine in a White Wine

Sauce Melt 2 tablespoons butter, then add 1 sliced red onion and cook over low heat for 15 minutes until very soft and lightly browned. Pour over 5 tablespoons dry white wine and cook for an additional 5–10 minutes until reduced down. Pour over ½ cup heavy cream and simmer for 1–2 minutes. Meanwhile, cook the chicken and fettuccine as above. Drain the pasta and stir through the chicken, cut into bite-size pieces, and wine sauce. Serve immediately.

30 Pasta Rolls with Red Pepper and Ricotta

Serves 4

8 dried lasagna sheets

2 cups ricotta cheese

¾ cup grated Parmesan cheese

2 roasted red peppers from a jar, drained and cut into strips

1½ cups store-bought tomato pasta sauce

oil, for greasing

10 cherry tomatoes, halved

salt

- Cook the lasagna sheets in a large saucepan of salted boiling water for 6 minutes, then drain. Cool under cold running water and drain again.

- Spread ricotta over a lasagna sheet and sprinkle with a little of the Parmesan. Arrange a couple of strips of red pepper on top, then roll up tightly to form a tube. Cut into small cylinders, about ¾ inch long. Repeat with the remaining lasagna sheets.

- Pour the tomato pasta sauce over a large, lightly greased ovenproof dish. Arrange the pasta rolls on top. Tuck the tomatoes into any gaps, then sprinkle with the remaining Parmesan.

- Place in a preheated oven, 400°F, for 15 minutes or until the pasta is soft and the sauce is bubbling.

 Easy Red Pepper and Ricotta Pasta Salad Cook 1 lb fresh conchiglie according to the package instructions until al dente. Meanwhile, place 2 drained roasted red peppers from a jar, 2 seeded tomatoes, 1 crushed garlic clove, a handful of basil leaves and 3 tablespoons extra virgin olive oil in a food processor or blender and whiz together. Drain the pasta, then tip into a serving dish and stir through the red pepper sauce. Serve with ½ cup ricotta cheese dolloped over.

 Pasta Rolls with Zucchini and Ricotta Make the recipe as above, replacing the red peppers with 2 zucchini, cut into thin strips. Rub the zucchini strips with 2 tablespoons olive oil, then cook under a preheated medium broiler for 2–3 minutes on each side until lightly charred and soft. Arrange on the lasagna sheets with the cheese and then cook as above.

Farfalle with Chicken Corn Bites and Red Pepper Sauce

Serves 4

10 oz ground chicken

2 scallions, finely chopped

1 egg yolk

½ cup fresh white bread crumbs

¼ cup frozen corn kernels, thawed

4 tablespoons olive oil, plus extra for greasing

14 oz farfalle

3 ready-roasted red peppers

handful of basil leaves, chopped, plus extra to garnish (optional)

salt and pepper

- Mix together the chicken, scallions, egg yolk, bread crumbs, and corn in a bowl, then season well with salt and pepper. Lightly wet your hands, then shape the mixture into small balls, each about the size of a walnut.

- Place the chicken balls on a greased baking sheet and drizzle over 1 tablespoon of the oil. Place in a preheated oven, 400°F, for 12–15 minutes, turn once, until cooked through.

- Meanwhile, cook the pasta in a saucepan of salted boiling water according to the package instructions until al dente.

- Place the red peppers, 2 tablespoons of the oil, and the basil in a food processor or blender and whiz together to form a chunky sauce. Drain the pasta, reserving a little of the cooking water, and return to the pan. Stir through the remaining oil and the red pepper sauce, adding a little cooking water to loosen if needed. Spoon into bowls, add the chicken bites, sprinkle with some basil and serve.

 Chicken, Corn, and Red Pepper Pasta Salad Cook 10 oz orzo according to the package instructions, adding ½ cup canned corn kernels 1 minute before the end of the cooking time. Drain, cool under cold running water, and drain again. Tip into a serving dish and mix with 1 store-bought roasted chicken breast, skin discarded and flesh torn into shreds, 5 tablespoons mayonnaise, 1 cored, seeded, and chopped red bell pepper, and a handful of chopped basil leaves.

 Chicken and Corn Farfalle with Red Pepper Sauce Heat 4 tablespoons olive oil in a skillet, add 2 sliced garlic cloves, and cook for 30 seconds. Stir in 4 cored, seeded, and chopped red bell peppers, reduce the heat to low, and cook for 15 minutes or until softened. Pour over ¾ cup pureed tomatoes and cook for an additional 10 minutes until thickened. Meanwhile, fry 2 seasoned boneless, skinless chicken breasts in a little olive oil for 7 minutes on each side or until golden and cooked through, then remove from the pan. Add ¼ cup frozen corn kernels, thawed, and cook for 1–2 minutes until lightly browned. Cut the chicken into slices. While the peppers and chicken are cooking, cook and drain the farfalle as above. Stir through the chicken slices and red pepper sauce, then serve topped with the corn and sprinkled with chopped basil leaves.

30 Seafood Spaghetti in a Creamy Sauce

Serves 4

1 tablespoon butter
1 shallot, finely chopped
6 tablespoons dry vermouth
¾ cup hot fish stock
10 oz salmon fillet
3 oz small cooked unpeeled
  shrimp
12 scallops, corals removed
⅔ cup heavy cream
handful of chives, chopped, plus
  extra to garnish
14 oz spaghetti
salt and pepper

- Melt the butter in a saucepan, add the shallot, and cook for 3 minutes until softened. Pour over the vermouth and bubble for 5 minutes until reduced by half. Add the stock, then place the salmon in the pan, making sure it is covered with liquid, and gently poach for 5–10 minutes or until the fish is cooked through and flakes easily. Remove from the pan, discard the skin, and flake into bite-size pieces.

- Add the shrimp to the pan, then add the scallops and cook for an additional 2 minutes or until just cooked through. Set aside with the salmon.

- Add the cream to the pan and bubble until reduced down to a sauce, then season with salt and pepper. Carefully stir in the reserved seafood, heat through and add the chives.

- Meanwhile, cook the pasta in a large saucepan of salted boiling water according to the package instructions until al dente. Drain, then toss through the seafood sauce and season. Serve sprinkled with extra chopped chives.

---

1 Simple Seafood Spaghetti

Cook the spaghetti as above. Add 7 oz large raw peeled shrimp 3 minutes and ⅔ cup frozen peas to the pan 2–3 minutes before the end of the cooking time and cook until the shrimp turn pink and are cooked through and the peas are tender. Drain well and return to the pan, then stir through 6 tablespoons sour cream and a handful of chopped dill weed. Serve at once.

2 Seafood Spaghetti with Prosciutto

Cook the spaghetti as above. Meanwhile, melt a little butter in a large skillet, add 4 sliced scallions, and cook for a couple of minutes until softened. Add 8 large scallops, corals removed, and a handful of large raw peeled shrimp, season, and cook over medium-high heat for 2 minutes on each side or until the shrimp have turned pink and the scallops are golden. Remove from the pan. Stir in a splash of dry white wine and bubble until reduced, then add 6 tablespoons heavy cream and mix in the seafood to warm through. Heat 1 teaspoon olive oil in a separate skillet, add 2 slices of prosciutto and cook for 1–2 minutes or until browned. Drain the pasta and stir into the seafood sauce, then crumble over the prosciutto. Serve immediately.

Chicken Parmigiana with Tomato Fusilli Lunghi

Serves 4

2 cups fresh white bread crumbs

¼ cup Grated Parmesan cheese

4 tablespoons olive oil, plus extra for greasing

4 small boneless, skinless chicken breasts

3 oz mozzarella cheese, cut into 4 slices

10 oz fusilli lunghi

1 cup store-bought tomato pasta sauce

salt and pepper

green salad, to serve

· Mix together the bread crumbs and Parmesan on a large plate and season. Rub about 2 teaspoons of the oil over each chicken breast, press down with your palm to flatten a little, then dip in the bread crumb mixture until coated all over. Place on a lightly greased broiler pan.

· Drizzle with a little more oil, then cook under a preheated hot broiler for 10 minutes, turning once, until golden and cooked through. Top each chicken breast with a slice of mozzarella and cook for an additional 2 minutes or until the cheese has melted.

· Meanwhile, cook the pasta in a large saucepan of salted boiling water according to the package instructions until al dente. Heat the tomato pasta sauce in a small saucepan. Drain the pasta and toss through the sauce. Cut each chicken breast in half. Spoon into serving bowls and top with the grilled chicken. Serve with the green salad.

10 Easy Chicken, Mozzarella, and Tomato Spaghetti Heat 1 tablespoon olive oil in a wok or large skillet, add 10 oz stir-fry chicken tenders, and stir-fry for 7 minutes or until just cooked through. Pour over 1 cup store-bought tomato pasta sauce and simmer for 1–2 minutes. Meanwhile, cook 14 oz spaghetti according to the package instructions until al dente. Drain and return to the pan. Cut 3 oz mozzarella cheese into small chunks and stir through the pasta with the chicken sauce. Serve immediately.

30 Chicken, Mozzarella, and Tomato Pasta Bake Cook 14 oz fusilli according to the package instructions until al dente. Drain and return to the pan. Toss through 1 cup store-bought tomato pasta sauce and 2 store-bought roasted chicken breasts, skin discarded and flesh cut into bite-size pieces. Tip into an ovenproof dish. Mix together ⅔ cup sour cream with enough milk to make a sauce, then drizzle over the top of the pasta. Sprinkle with 1 cup grated mozzarella and place in a preheated oven, 400°F, for 15 minutes or until golden and bubbling.

Creamy Mustard and Sausage Pasta

Serves 4

2 tablespoons olive oil
6 pork sausages
1 onion, thickly sliced
2 teaspoons whole grain mustard
⅔ cup hot vegetable or chicken
  stock
5 tablespoons sour cream
juice and grated zest of ½ lemon
14 oz chifferi pasta
salt
chopped flat-leaf parsley,
  to garnish

- Brush a little oil over each sausage, then cook under a preheated medium broiler for 15 minutes or until golden and cooked through. Cool slightly, then cut into bite-size pieces.

- Meanwhile, heat the remaining oil in a pan, add the onion, and cook for 10 minutes until softened. Stir in the mustard and stock and simmer for 5 minutes, then stir in the sour cream and lemon juice and most of the zest.

- While the sausages and sauce are cooking, cook the pasta in a large saucepan of salted boiling water according to the package instructions until al dente. Drain, reserving a little of the cooking water, and return to the pan. Stir through the sausages and sauce, adding a little cooking water to loosen if needed.

- Spoon into serving bowls and serve sprinkled with the parsley and the remaining lemon zest.

 Quick Mustard and Pancetta Pasta

Cook and drain the chifferi pasta as above. Meanwhile, heat a little olive oil in a skillet, add 5 oz pancetta cubes and 2 sliced garlic cloves, and cook for 5 minutes. Stir in 2 teaspoons whole grain mustard and 5 tablespoons sour cream. Stir through the drained pasta and serve as above.

 Slow-Cooked Onion and Mustardy Sausage Pasta

Heat a little olive oil in a skillet, add 1 sliced red onion and cook over low heat for 20–25 minutes until soft and golden. Meanwhile, broil the sausages as above and cut into bite-size pieces. Stir into the onion with 1 chopped garlic clove, a splash of dry white wine, 1 chopped sage leaf, and 2 teaspoons whole grain mustard. Simmer for 5 minutes, then stir in 2 tablespoons sour cream. Meanwhile, cook and drain the chifferi pasta as above. Stir through the sauce and serve immediately.

Simple One-Pan Tomato Pasta

Serves 4

4 tablespoons olive oil
12 oz garganelli pasta
thyme sprig, leaves stripped and
　chopped
4 tablespoons tomato paste
2 teaspoons red wine vinegar
6 cups hot chicken stock
pinch of superfine sugar
½ cup cherry tomatoes, halved
salt and pepper
chopped basil leaves, to garnish
Parmesan cheese shavings,
　to serve

- Heat the oil in a large, deep flameproof casserole, add the pasta, and toss around the pan for a couple of minutes until golden. Add the thyme, tomato paste, and vinegar and stir in to coat the pasta.

- Add a ladleful of stock and the sugar to the pan. Keeping the sauce at a gentle simmer, add the stock, one ladleful at a time, stirring occasionally.

- After 10 minutes cooking, add the tomatoes. Cook for an additional 5–10 minutes until the liquid has been absorbed or the pasta is tender. Season well with salt and pepper and serve sprinkled with the basil and Parmesan shavings.

 Penne with Sundried Tomato and Basil Pesto Cook 14 oz penne according to the package instructions until al dente. Meanwhile, place 1 cup drained sundried tomatoes in oil, 2 crushed garlic cloves, ¼ cup toasted pine nuts, 1 teaspoon balsamic vinegar, 3 tablespoons extra virgin olive oil and a handful of basil leaves in a food processor or blender and whiz together to form a pesto. Drain the pasta, reserving a little of the cooking water, and return to the pan. Stir through the pesto, adding a little cooking water to loosen if needed. Serve immediately.

 Slow-Cooked Tomato Pasta Halve and seed 8 oz plum tomatoes. Place in a large skillet with ½ cup olive oil and 3 garlic cloves and cook over very low heat for 20–25 minutes until soft and just about to fall apart. Season well. Meanwhile, cook and drain the garganelli as above. Stir through the tomatoes with a handful of chopped basil leaves and a handful of grated Parmesan cheese. Serve immediately.

 # Easy Sausage Spaghetti Bolognese

Serves 4

1 tablespoon olive oil
6 garlic sausages
1 onion, finely chopped
5 oz button mushrooms, quartered
1 teaspoon tomato paste
13 oz can chopped tomatoes
handful of basil leaves, finely chopped
½ cup water
14 oz spaghetti
salt and pepper
grated Parmesan cheese, to serve

- Heat a large skillet until hot, then add the oil. Remove the sausages from their casings and crumble the sausagemeat into the pan. Cook for a couple of minutes, breaking up the meat with the back of a spoon. When it begins to brown, add the onion and cook for an additional 5 minutes. Stir in the mushrooms and cook until they begin to soften.

- Stir in the tomato paste, tomatoes, basil, and measurement water. Bring to a boil, then reduce the heat and simmer for 10 minutes or until cooked through. Season well with salt and pepper.

- Meanwhile, cook the pasta in a large saucepan of salted boiling water according to the package instructions until al dente, then drain. Spoon into serving bowls and top with the sausage sauce. Serve sprinkled with the Parmesan.

 Simple Bacon Spaghetti Bolognese Cook and drain the spaghetti as above. Meanwhile, heat a little olive oil in a skillet, add 3 finely sliced bacon slices and cook for 1–2 minutes. Pour over 1½ store-bought Bolognese pasta sauce, then stir in 1 cup ready-cooked Puy lentils. Simmer for 5 minutes, then toss through the drained pasta. Serve immediately.

Sausage Meatball Spaghetti Bolognese Remove the sausages from their casings as above and place in a bowl. Lightly wet your hands, then shape the sausagemeat into small balls. Cook in the oil as above, adding the onion, but omitting the mushrooms. Stir in 5 tablespoons dry white wine and simmer until nearly cooked away, then add the tomato paste, tomatoes, and measurement water and continue as above.

30 Skillet Macaroni and Cheese

Serves 4

11 oz elbow macaroni
3½ tablespoons butter
6 tablespoons all-purpose flour
2½ cups milk
1 cup grated cheddar cheese
1 oz dried white bread crumbs
¼ cup grated Parmesan cheese
salt and pepper

- Cook the pasta in a large saucepan of salted boiling water according to the package instructions until al dente.

- Meanwhile, melt the butter in a large, ovenproof skillet and stir in the flour to make a smooth paste. Cook until golden, then gradually whisk in the milk. Bring to a boil over medium heat, then simmer for about 3 minutes until slightly thickened. Remove from the heat, stir in the cheese, and season with salt and pepper.

- Drain the pasta, then tip into the skillet. Stir into the cheese sauce until well combined. Sprinkle with the bread crumbs and Parmesan.

- Place in a preheated oven, 375°F, for 15 minutes or until golden brown and bubbling.

1 Pasta in a Cheesy Sauce Cook 14 oz chifferi pasta according to the package instructions until al dente. Meanwhile, place 1 garlic clove and 6 tablespoons heavy cream in a saucepan and cook for 5 minutes. Remove and discard the garlic and stir in ½ cup grated Parmesan cheese. Drain the pasta and return to the pan. Stir through the sauce and serve immediately.

2 Creamy Macaroni and Cheese Melt a little butter in a saucepan, add 1 finely chopped shallot and cook until softened. Pour over 5 tablespoons dry white wine and cook for 5–10 minutes until reduced down. Stir through ⅔ cup sour cream and enough milk to make a smooth sauce. Meanwhile, cook and drain the macaroni as above. Tip into a heatproof dish and stir through the sauce. Sprinkle with ½ cup grated Gruyère cheese and cook under a preheated medium broiler for 7 minutes or until golden and bubbling.

10 Tagliarelle with Pesto and Charred Tomatoes

Serves 4

1 cup cherry tomatoes
1 tablespoon olive oil
14 oz tagliarelle
5 tablespoons store-bought fresh
   green pesto
3 tablespoons mascarpone
   cheese
2 tablespoons toasted pine nuts
salt and pepper

- Place the cherry tomatoes on a baking sheet, then mix together with the oil and season. Cook under a preheated medium broiler for 5 minutes or until beginning to brown.

- Meanwhile, cook the pasta in a large saucepan of salted boiling water according to the package instructions until al dente. Drain, reserving a little of the cooking water, and return to the pan. Stir through the pesto and mascarpone, adding a little cooking water to loosen if needed.

- Gently stir in the tomatoes and season. Spoon into serving bowls and serve with the pine nuts sprinkled over.

20 Tomato Tagliarelle with Pesto-stuffed Chicken Mix together 4 tablespoons store-bought fresh green pesto and 2 tablespoons mascarpone cheese in a bowl, then spoon under the skin of 4 boneless chicken breasts. Place in a roasting pan and drizzle with olive oil. Place in a preheated oven, 425°F, and cook for 15 minutes. Add a handful of cherry tomatoes, return to the oven, and cook for an additional 5 minutes or until the chicken is cooked through and the tomatoes have softened. Meanwhile, cook and drain 10 oz tagliarelle as above, then stir through the tomatoes and 3 tablespoons mascarpone. Serve with the chicken.

30 Mexican-Style Tagliarelle with Spicy Tomato Pesto Heat a little olive oil in a skillet, add 1 sliced onion and cook over low heat for 10 minutes until softened. Drain a 13 oz can cannellini beans and add to the onion. Pour over 6 tablespoons hot chicken stock and simmer for 15 minutes until all the liquid has been absorbed. Meanwhile, place ¼ cup pumpkin seeds, 1 jalapeno chili, 2 drained sundried tomatoes in oil, a handful of cilantro leaves and a squeeze of lime juice in a small food processor or blender and whiz together to form a pesto. Cook and drain the tagliarelle as above. Stir through the beans and 3 tablespoons sour cream. Serve topped with the pesto.

30 Broccoli and Ham Pasta Bake

Serves 4

14 oz spirali
4 oz tenderstem broccoli
1¾ cups hot chicken or vegetable
   stock
1 teaspoon mustard
¾ cup sour cream
5 oz ham, cut into bite-size
   pieces
1 cup grated cheddar cheese
salt and pepper

- Cook the pasta in a large saucepan of salted boiling water according to the package instructions until al dente. Add the broccoli 5 minutes before the end of the cooking time and cook until just tender. Drain and return to the pan.

- Meanwhile, stir together the stock, mustard, and sour cream in a bowl, then mix together with the pasta, broccoli, ham and half the cheddar and season. Spoon into an ovenproof dish and sprinkle with the remaining cheese.

- Place in a preheated oven, 400°F, for 15 minutes or until golden, bubbling, and cooked through.

10 Quick Broccoli and Ham Cavatappi

Cook 1 lb fresh cavatappi according to the package instructions until al dente, adding the broccoli as above. Meanwhile, heat a little olive oil in a skillet, add 1 garlic clove, and cook for 30 seconds. Pour over ⅔ cup pureed tomato and simmer for 5 minutes. Drain the pasta and broccoli and return to the pan. Stir through the tomato sauce and the ham as above and serve sprinkled with grated Parmesan cheese.

20 Ham, Broccoli, and Spirali Gratin

Cook the spirali and broccoli as above, adding 5 cups baby spinach leaves to the pan just before draining. Drain the pasta and vegetables and return to the pan. Mix together with ¾ cup hot chicken or vegetable stock and the sour cream and ham as above. Tip into a heatproof dish and sprinkle with 4 oz sliced mozzarella. Cook under a preheated medium broiler for 5–10 minutes or until golden and bubbling.

Salmon and Leek Conchiglie

Serves 4

2 x 5 oz salmon fillets
2 tablespoons butter
2 leeks, trimmed, cleaned, and
  finely sliced
juice and grated zest of 1 lemon
14 oz conchiglie
3 tablespoons sour cream
salt and pepper

- Place the salmon fillets in a skillet and pour over enough water to cover. Bring to a boil, then reduce the heat and simmer for 10 minutes or until the fish is cooked through and flakes easily. Remove the skin and any bones and use a fork to break into large chunks.

- Meanwhile, heat the butter in a small saucepan, add the leeks, and cook over gentle heat for 10 minutes or until softened and cooked through. Stir in the lemon juice and most of the zest.

- Cook the pasta in a large saucepan of salted boiling water according to the package instructions until al dente. Drain, reserving a little of the cooking water, and return to the pan. Stir through the salmon and leeks and season with salt and pepper, then stir in the sour cream, adding a little cooking water if needed to make a sauce. Serve immediately with plenty of black pepper and the remaining lemon zest sprinkled over.

 Simple Salmon and Leek Conchiglie

Cook 1 lb fresh conchiglie according to the package instructions until al dente. Add the leeks, prepared as above, to the pan 3 minutes before the end of the cooking time and cook until softened. Drain and return to the pan. Stir in 5 oz sliced smoked salmon with the sour cream and lemon juice as above. Serve immediately.

 Salmon, Smoked Haddock, and Leek

Pasta Bake Poach 1 smoked haddock fillet and 1 salmon fillet ¾ cup milk for 10 minutes or until the fish is cooked through and flakes easily. Remove any skin and bones and flake into small pieces. Meanwhile, cook the leeks and pasta as above, adding 4½ cups baby spinach leaves to the pasta just before draining. Stir in the fish and poaching liquid, leeks, and 3 tablespoons sour cream, then spoon into an ovenproof dish. Sprinkle over ½ cups fresh white bread crumbs and dab over a little butter, then place in a preheated oven, 400°F, for 15 minutes or until golden and cooked through.

Tuna and Corn Pasta Bake

Serves 4

3 tablespoons butter
5 tablespoons all-purpose flour
2½ cups milk
14 oz fusilli
2 x 6½ oz cans tuna in spring
   water, drained
7 oz can corn kernels, drained
¾ cups grated cheddar cheese
¼ cup dried white bread crumbs
salt and pepper

- Melt the butter in a medium-sized saucepan and stir in the flour to make a smooth paste. Cook until golden, then gradually whisk in the milk. Bring to a boil, stirring constantly, then reduce the heat and simmer for 10 minutes until thickened, stirring occasionally. Season well with salt and pepper.

- Meanwhile, cook the pasta in a large saucepan of salted boiling water according to the package instructions until al dente. Drain and return to the pan. Mix in the white sauce, tuna, corn, and the cheddar, reserving a little for the topping.

- Spoon into a medium ovenproof dish and sprinkle with the bread crumbs and reserved cheese. Place in a preheated oven, 400°F, for 15 minutes or until lightly browned and bubbling.

---

1 **Tuna and Corn Pasta Salad** Cook 10 oz fusilli as above. Drain, then cool under cold running water and drain again. Tip into a serving dish and stir through 6 tablespoons mayonnaise, a drained 6½ oz can tuna in spring water and 4 oz drained canned corn kernels.

2 **Creamy Corn and Bacon Fusilli** Heat a little olive oil in a skillet, add 1 finely chopped onion and cook until beginning to soften. Cut 4 bacon slices into small pieces, add to the pan, and cook for 5–7 minutes or until the bacon is golden and cooked through. Pour over 6 tablespoons hot vegetable stock and cook for an additional 5 minutes until beginning to reduce. Add a drained 7 oz can corn kernels and 3 tablespoons heavy cream and cook for 5 minutes or until the corn is cooked through. Meanwhile, cook and drain the fusilli as above. Stir through the sauce with ¼ cup grated cheddar cheese. Serve immediately.

 # Linguine Fiorentina with Ham

Serves 4

1 tablespoon olive oil
1 onion, finely chopped
2 garlic cloves, finely chopped
4½ cups spinach leaves, chopped
5 tablespoons low-fat sour cream
handful of grated Parmesan
   cheese, plus extra to serve
14 oz linguine
4 oz smoked ham, sliced
salt and pepper

- Heat the oil in a skillet, add the onion and garlic, and cook for 5 minutes until softened.

- Place the spinach in a colander over the sink and pour over enough boiling water until just wilted. Squeeze out any excess water. Place in a food processor or blender with the onion and garlic, sour cream, and Parmesan and whiz together to form a thick paste. Set aside.

- Cook the pasta in a large saucepan of salted boiling water according to the package instructions until al dente. Drain, reserving a little of the cooking water, and return to the pan. Stir through the spinach mixture, adding a little cooking water to loosen.

- Stir through the ham and season with salt and pepper. Spoon into serving bowls and serve sprinkled with extra Parmesan.

 ### Mushroom, Spinach, and Ham

Linguine Heat a little olive oil in a skillet, add 1 sliced garlic clove and 5 oz mixed wild mushrooms, trimmed and halved if large, and cook for 3 minutes until soft. Cook the linguine as above, adding 4½ cups baby spinach leaves just before draining. Drain and return to the pan. Stir through the mushrooms, 4 oz sliced ham, and 3 tablespoons sour cream. Serve as above.

 ### Linguine Fiorentina Ham and Egg Bakes

Cook the recipe as above, then divide the mixture between 4 large individual soufflé dishes. Crack an egg over each one and top with a little butter. Place in a preheated oven, 350°F, for 10 minutes or until the eggs are just cooked through. Serve immediately.

30 Spinach and Ricotta Cannelloni

Serves 4

5 cups spinach leaves
handful of basil leaves
2 cups ricotta cheese
½ cup grated Parmesan cheese
pinch of grated nutmeg
2 cups store-bought tomato
　pasta sauce
8 fresh lasagna sheets
4 oz mozzarella cheese, thinly
　sliced
salt and pepper
green salad, to serve (optional)

- Place the spinach in a colander over the sink and pour over enough boiling water until just wilted. Squeeze out any excess water. Roughly chop the spinach and basil, place in a bowl and mix together with the ricotta, half the Parmesan, and the nutmeg. Season to taste with salt and pepper.

- Heat the tomato pasta sauce in a small saucepan until simmering.

- Prepare the lasagna sheets, if necessary, according to the package instructions. Spread about a third of the tomato sauce over the bottom of a medium ovenproof dish. Spoon 2–3 tablespoons of the spinach mixture along the length of each sheet. Roll up and place in the dish. Pour over the remaining tomato sauce and arrange the mozzarella on top.

- Sprinkle with the remaining Parmesan and place in a preheated oven, 400°F, for 15–20 minutes until the cheese is golden. Serve with green salad, if desired.

 Spinach Spaghetti with Ricotta

Cook 14 oz spaghetti according to the package instructions until al dente. Drain and return to the pan. Toss through 4½ cups spinach, chopped, 4 tablespoons store-bought fresh green pesto, and a handful of halved baby plum tomatoes. Top with dollops of ricotta cheese and serve with grated Parmesan cheese, if desired.

 Quick Spinach and Ricotta Lasagna

Cook 8 fresh lasagna sheets in a large saucepan of salted boiling water for 3–5 minutes or until soft, then drain well. Prepare 2¼ cups spinach leaves as above, drain well, then finely chop and mix together with half the tomato pasta sauce and 3 tablespoons store-bought fresh green pesto. Spoon a layer of the spinach mixture into a heatproof dish and cover with a layer of lasagna sheets. Spoon 1 cup ricotta on top, then cover with another layer of pasta. Pour over the remaining tomato sauce, grate over 1 oz Parmesan cheese, and cook under a preheated medium broiler for 10 minutes or until golden and cooked through.

30 Hearty Sausage and Spinach Pasta Bake

Serves 4

6 large pork sausages
1 tablespoon olive oil
2 cups store-bought tomato
  pasta sauce
10 oz penne
4½ cups baby spinach leaves
1 cup ricotta cheese
¾ cup mascarpone cheese
5 tablespoons milk
4 oz mozzarella cheese, torn
salt and pepper

- Squeeze the sausages out of their casings into a bowl. Lightly wet your hands, then shape the sausagemeat into tiny meatballs. Heat the oil in a skillet, add the sausage balls, and cook for about 5 minutes, stirring frequently, until golden all over. Pour over the tomato pasta sauce and simmer for 5 minutes.

- Meanwhile, cook the pasta in a large saucepan of salted boiling water according to the package instructions until al dente. Remove from the heat, add the spinach leaves and then drain, reserving a little of the cooking water, and return to the pan.

- Mix together the ricotta, mascarpone, and milk in a bowl, then stir through the pasta and season well with salt and pepper.

- Spoon the tomato and sausage sauce into a medium ovenproof dish. Arrange the pasta on top and cover with the mozzarella. Place in a preheated oven, 375°F, for 15 minutes or until golden, bubbling, and cooked through.

1 Bacon and Spinach Penne

Cook 4 bacon slices under a preheated medium broiler for 7 minutes or until crisp. Cool for 1 minute, then cut into small pieces. Meanwhile, cook and drain the penne and spinach as above. Toss together with the bacon and 2 chopped tomatoes. Mix 1 cup ricotta cheese with 2 oz feta cheese in a bowl and spoon over the pasta. Serve immediately.

2 Penne with Sausages and Spinach

Heat 2 tablespoons olive oil in a skillet, add 1 sliced garlic clove and cook for 30 seconds. Pour over a 13 oz can chopped tomatoes and a pinch each of dried red pepper flakes and dried oregano. Simmer for 15 minutes until thickened. Meanwhile, cook 6 large pork sausages under a preheated medium broiler for 15 minutes or until cooked through. Cool slightly, then cut into bite-size pieces and heat through in the sauce. Meanwhile, cook and drain the pasta and spinach as above. Toss together with the sausage sauce and then spoon over ½ cup ricotta cheese. Serve immediately.

QuickCook
Healthy
Suppers

Recipes listed by cooking time

3O

2O

Fresh Pasta Broth with Onion Garnish

Serves 4

2 tablespoons olive oil

2 onions, 1 finely chopped and 1 thinly sliced

2 garlic cloves, finely chopped

large handful of mint leaves, chopped

½ teaspoon turmeric

¾ cup canned chickpeas, drained and rinsed

¾ cup canned kidney beans, drained and rinsed

6 cups hot chicken stock

4 oz fine egg noodles, broken into small pieces

⅔ cup frozen peas

1 cup chopped greens, cilantro and flat-leaf parsley, to serve

4 tablespoons plain yogurt

- To make the onion garnish, heat half the oil in a small skillet, add the thinly sliced onion, and cook gently for 10 minutes until softened and lightly golden. Add the garlic and mint and cook for a minute more.

- Meanwhile, heat the oil in a large saucepan, add the chopped onion, and cook for a couple of minutes until softened. Stir in the turmeric, then add the chickpeas and kidney beans and stir in the stock. Bring to a boil and cook for a couple of minutes. Add the pasta and cook for an additional 5 minutes.

- Add the peas and greens to the soup, season with salt and pepper, and cook for 2–3 minutes or until the vegetables are tender and the pasta is cooked through.

- Ladle into serving bowls, sprinkle over the onion garnish and chopped herbs, then drizzle with the yogurt. Serve with pita breads.

Quick Pasta Broth with Caramelized

Onion Fry 1 teaspoon curry paste in a large saucepan for a couple of seconds, then add 4 tablespoons shop-bought ready-cooked fried onion, pour over the stock as above and bring to the boil. Add 13 oz rinsed and drained can chickpeas and the noodles, prepared as above, and simmer until the pasta is cooked. Add the greens and peas 2–3 minutes before the end of cooking time. Serve topped with cooked caramelized onion.

Spicy Pasta Pilaff with Crispy Fried

Onion Heat 1 tablespoon olive oil in a large saucepan, add 1 chopped onion, and fry gently until softened. Stir in 1 teaspoon ground cumin and a pinch of turmeric. Add ½ cup long grain rice and 2 cups angel hair pasta. Coat in the spices, then pour over 2 cups hot chicken stock and add ¾ cup rinsed and drained canned chickpeas. Bring to a boil, then cover with a lid and simmer for 15–20 minutes or until the rice is just cooked through. Meanwhile, heat a saucepan one-third full of vegetable oil. When hot, fry 1 sliced onion until crisp and browned. Remove with a slotted spoon and serve sprinkled over the pilaff with chopped mint leaves.

30 Turkey Meatball and Pasta Soup

Serves 4

1 lb ground turkey
10 cup fresh white bread crumbs
¼ cup grated Parmesan cheese,
  plus extra to serve (optional)
2 tablespoons finely chopped
  flat-leaf parsley, plus extra
  to garnish
1 egg, lightly beaten
1 garlic clove, crushed
6 cups hot chicken stock
2 large carrots, peeled and
  thinly sliced
6 oz farfalline pasta
salt and pepper

- Mix together the turkey, bread crumbs, Parmesan, parsley, egg, and garlic in a large bowl and season to taste with salt and pepper. Lightly wet your hands, then shape the mixture into small balls about ¾ inch round.

- Bring the stock to a boil in a large saucepan, then add the carrots and simmer for 5 minutes.

- Drop the turkey meatballs into the stock and cook for 5 minutes. Add the pasta and cook for an additional 5–7 minutes or until the meatballs are cooked through. Season to taste.

- Ladle into bowls and serve sprinkled with a little Parmesan and chopped parsley, if desired.

---

10 Simple Turkey Soup

Bring 4 cups hot chicken stock to a boil, then add 2 peeled and grated carrots and cook for 3 minutes. Stir in the pasta as above and cook for 5–7 minutes or until cooked through, adding 7 oz shredded cooked turkey slices 1 minute before the end of the cooking time to heat through. Serve sprinkled with finely chopped dill weed.

20 Grilled Turkey Steaks with Orzo

Dust 4 turkey steaks with a little flour and shake off any excess. Dip into 1 lightly beaten egg. Sprinkle 1 cup dried white bread crumbs and ¼ cup grated Parmesan cheese on a plate, then dip in the steaks to coat all over. Brush with a little olive oil and cook under a preheated medium broiler for 5–7 minutes on each side or until golden and cooked through. Meanwhile, cut 4 slices of pancetta into matchsticks.

Heat a little olive oil in a skillet and cook for 5 minutes or until golden. Remove from the pan. Tip 1 finely chopped shallot and 1 crushed garlic clove into the skillet and cook until softened. Cook 1 cup thinly sliced carrots for 10 minutes until tender, then add 14 oz orzo to the pan and cook according to the package instructions. Drain and toss together with the pancetta and onion mixture, and serve alongside the turkey steaks.

Arugula, Chili, and Ricotta Spaghetti

Serves 4

14 oz spaghetti
1 tablespoon olive oil
1 garlic clove, finely chopped
1 red chili, seeded if desired,
   and finely sliced
4½ cups arugula leaves
⅔ cup ricotta cheese
salt and pepper

- Cook the pasta in a large saucepan of salted boiling water according to the pack instructions until al dente.

- Meanwhile, heat the oil in a small frying pan, add the garlic and chilli and cook for 30 seconds until beginning to brown. Remove from the heat.

- Drain the pasta, reserving a little of the cooking water, and return to the pan. Stir through the chilli oil, adding a little cooking water to loosen if needed. Season well.

- Stir through the rocket, spoon into serving bowls and top with the ricotta. Serve immediately.

 Spaghetti with Creamy Ricotta and Salad Leaves Melt 2 tablespoons butter in a sauce pan and stir in 4 tablespoons all-purpose flour to make a smooth paste. Cook until golden, then gradually whisk in 1¼ cups milk, stirring frequently, and simmer for 5–10 minutes until thickened. Stir in ⅔ cup ricotta cheese and a handful of grated Parmesan cheese. Meanwhile, cook and drain the spaghetti as above. Stir through the ricotta sauce and 4¼ cups mixed baby spinach, arugula, and watercress leaves. Serve immediately sprinkled with dried red pepper flakes.

 Ricotta Pasta Bakes with Spicy Arugula Salad Cook 12 oz angel hair pasta according to the package instructions. Drain, then cool under cold running water and drain again. Snip into small strips and mix together with 6 beaten eggs and ⅔ cup ricotta cheese in a bowl. Grease 12 cups of a muffin pan, then divide the mixture between the cups. Place in a preheated oven, 400°F, for 15–20 minutes or until just cooked through. Toss together the arugula and chili, prepared as above, 1 teaspoon white wine vinegar, and 2 tablespoons extra virgin olive oil in a bowl and serve alongside the pasta bakes.

PAS-HEAL-BUD

Fettuccine with Goats' Cheese and Tomato Salsa

Serves 4

14 oz fettuccine
4 oz soft goat cheese
3 tablespoons low-fat cream
  cheese
salt and pepper

For the tomato salsa

¾ cup baby plum
  tomatoes, halved
5 sundried tomatoes in oil,
  drained and finely chopped
1 tablespoon balsamic vinegar
1 tablespoon extra virgin olive oil
handful of basil leaves, chopped

- To make the tomato salsa, stir together the tomatoes, vinegar, oil, and basil in a bowl. Season well with salt and pepper and allow to stand for 5 minutes.

- Meanwhile, cook the pasta in a large saucepan of salted boiling water according to the package instructions until al dente.

- Drain the pasta, reserving a little of the cooking water, and return to the pan. Stir through the cheeses, adding a little cooking water to loosen. Season well.

- Spoon onto serving plates and serve topped with the tomato salsa and basil leaves.

 Fettuccine with Goat Cheese and Roasted Tomatoes
Place ¾ cup cherry tomatoes in a roasting pan and drizzle over a little olive oil. Place in a preheated oven, 350°F, for 15 minutes or until cooked through. Sprinkle with a handful of chopped oregano leaves, a pinch of sugar, and 1 tablespoon balsamic vinegar 2 minutes before the end of the cooking time. Meanwhile, cook and drain the fettuccine as above, reserving a little of the cooking water. Stir through 4 oz soft goat cheese, 5 tablespoons mascarpone cheese, and a handful of grated Parmesan cheese, adding a little cooking water to loosen. Spoon into bowls and serve topped with the roasted tomatoes and a few toasted pine nuts.

 Goat Cheese Pasta Bake with Tomato Salsa Cook 14 oz penne according to the package instructions until al dente. Meanwhile, mix together the goat and cream cheeses with 3 tablespoons low-fat sour cream in a bowl. Thin with a little milk to make a sauce, then toss together with the drained pasta. Spoon into an ovenproof dish, top with a handful of grated Parmesan cheese, if desired, and bake in a preheated oven, 375°F, for 15–20 minutes or until bubbling and cooked through. Meanwhile, make the tomato salsa as above. Top the pasta with the salsa and serve immediately.

Open Butternut Squash and Ricotta Lasagne

Serves 4

1 red onion, sliced
½ butternut squash, peeled, seeded, and sliced
1 tablespoon olive oil
6 dried lasagna sheets
1 cup ricotta cheese
5 tablespoons mascarpone cheese
juice and grated zest of ½ lemon, plus extra zest to garnish
1¼ cups arugula leaves
salt

· Place the onion and butternut squash in a roasting pan and drizzle with the oil. Bake in a preheated oven, 425°F, for 15 minutes or until golden and softened.

· Meanwhile, cook the lasagna sheets in a large saucepan of boiling salted water for 7–10 minutes or until soft, then cut each sheet in half. While the pasta is cooking, mix together the ricotta, mascarpone and lemon juice and zest in a small bowl.

· Place 1 half-sheet of lasagna on each of 4 serving plates, top with some squash and onion, then add some of the ricotta mixture. Repeat the layers until all the pasta is used up. Sprinkle with the arugula and lemon zest and serve immediately.

 Speedy Butternut Squash and Ricotta Pasta Cook the squash, prepared as above and cut into cubes, and 14 oz penne in a saucepan of boiling water for 10 minutes. Drain, reserving a little of the cooking water, and return to the pan. Stir through 1 tablespoon mascarpone cheese, adding a little cooking water to loosen, then dollop over 1 cup ricotta cheese. Serve immediately.

 Butternut Squash and Ricotta Cannelloni Cook the squash, prepared as above, in a saucepan of boiling salted water for 10 minutes until soft, then drain well. Place in a food processor or blender and blend to a puree. Mix together with the ricotta and mascarpone cheeses as above. Spoon over 8 fresh lasagna sheets and roll up. Place in an ovenproof dish and pour over 1½ cups store-bought tomato pasta sauce and top with 1 cup grated mozzarella cheese. Place in a preheated oven, 400°F, for 15 minutes or until golden and cooked through.

10 Pasta Niçoise

Serves 4

14 oz ditalini
5 oz green beans, trimmed
7 oz can tuna in spring water,
  drained and flaked
½ cup cherry tomatoes,
  quartered
⅓ cup pitted black olives
  (preferably Niçoise)
2 cups arugula
salt

For the dressing

3 anchovy fillets in oil, drained
  and chopped
1 garlic clove, crushed
2 teaspoons white wine vinegar
2 tablespoons extra virgin olive oil

- Cook the pasta in a large saucepan of salted boiling water according to the package instructions until al dente. Add the beans 5 minutes before the end of the cooking time and cook until just tender.

- Meanwhile, make the dressing. Mash together the anchovies and garlic in a bowl, then mix in the vinegar and oil.

- Drain the pasta and beans, reserving a little of the cooking water, and return to the pan. Stir through the dressing, adding a little cooking water to loosen if needed. Mix through the remaining ingredients and serve immediately.

 Pasta Niçoise with Griddled Fiery Tuna Make the recipe as above, omitting the canned tuna. Meanwhile, rub 1 tablespoon olive oil and a pinch of dried red pepper flakes over 4 tuna steaks and season well with salt and pepper. Heat a griddle pan until smoking, add the tuna steaks, and cook for 3–5 minutes on each side, until browned on the outside but still rare inside. Slice the griddled tuna and add to the pasta.

 Pasta Niçoise with Red Pepper and Tomato Sauce Place 7 oz halved tomatoes and 1 halved, cored, and seeded red bell pepper in a roasting pan and drizzle with olive oil. Place in a preheated oven 400°F, for 20–25 minutes or until soft and lightly charred. Place in a food processor or blender with the tomatoes and pulse together to form a chunky sauce. Meanwhile, make the recipe as above. Drizzle the sauce on top of the pasta to serve.

1 Spaghetti with Kale and Gruyère

Serves 4

14 oz whole-wheat spaghetti
2 cups chopped kale
2 tablespoons olive oil
2 garlic cloves, sliced
1 tablespoon white wine vinegar
salt and pepper
1 oz Gruyère cheese, shaved,
  to serve

- Cook the pasta in a large saucepan of salted boiling water according to the package instructions until al dente. Add the kale 5 minutes before the end of the cooking time and cook until tender.

- Meanwhile, heat the oil in a skillet, add the garlic, and cook for 30 seconds until beginning to turn golden. Add the vinegar and cook for another couple of seconds. Remove from the heat.

- Drain the pasta and kale and return to the pan. Stir through the garlic oil and season with salt and pepper.

- Spoon into serving bowls and serve topped with shavings of Gruyère.

2 **Spaghetti with Slow-Cooked Kale and Gruyère** Heat a little olive oil in a large saucepan, add 1 sliced onion, and cook until softened. Add 1 chopped garlic clove and 2 cups chopped kale and cook for an additional 3 minutes, then reduce the heat and pour over 2 tablespoons water. Cover with a lid and cook for 15 minutes, adding more water if needed, until the kale is wilted and soft. Meanwhile, cook and drain the whole-wheat spaghetti as above. Toss through the kale and 2 chopped tomatoes and serve topped with Gruyère shavings as above.

3 **Kale and Butternut Squash Spaghetti with Gruyère** Toss ½ peeled, seeded, and cubed butternut squash with 2 tablespoons olive oil in a roasting pan. Place in a preheated oven 400°F for 20 minutes or until soft and golden. Meanwhile, cook and drain the whole-wheat spaghetti and kale as above. Pour 1½ cups store-bought tomato pasta sauce into a saucepan and heat through, then toss through the pasta with the kale and cooked squash. Serve topped with Gruyère shavings as above.

PAS-HEAL-QOE

Mushroom Tagliatelle Bolognese

Serves 4

10 oz mixed mushrooms, trimmed

2 tablespoons olive oil, plus extra
 to serve (optional)

1 onion, finely chopped

1 garlic clove, crushed

handful of thyme leaves

6 tablespoons dry white wine

1 teaspoon tomato paste

1¼ cups puréed tomatoes

14 oz tagliatelle

salt and pepper

grated Parmesan cheese,
 to serve

- Using a sharp knife, finely chop the mushrooms until they resemble bread crumbs. Alternatively, whiz the mushrooms in a food processor, being careful not to overprocess them so that they become mushy.

- Heat the oil in a large skillet, add the onion, mushrooms, garlic, and thyme and cook over a medium heat for 5 minutes, stirring frequently, until softened. Pour over the wine and cook for 5 minutes or until all the wine has been absorbed. Stir in the tomato paste and puréed tomatoes and simmer for an additional 10 minutes. Season to taste with salt and pepper.

- Meanwhile, cook the pasta in a large saucepan of salted boiling water according to the package instructions until al dente. Drain and return to the pan, then toss in a little olive oil, if desired, and stir through the sauce.

- Spoon into serving bowls and serve sprinkled with the Parmesan.

---

1 **Easy Mushroom Tagliatelle** Heat a little olive oil in a skillet, add 2 chopped garlic cloves, and cook for 1 minute until softened. Add 3 cups trimmed and sliced mushrooms and a pinch of dried reed pepper flakes and cook for another couple of minutes until softened. Meanwhile, cook and drain the tagliatelle as above. Toss the mushrooms, 3 chopped tomatoes, and a handful of chopped basil leaves through the drained pasta and serve immediately.

2 **Wild Mushroom Tagliatelle with Porcini Sauce** Soak 1 oz dried porcini mushrooms in ¼ cup boiling water for 15 minutes until softened. Meanwhile, heat a little olive oil in a skillet, add 1 chopped onion and 1 chopped garlic clove and fry gently until very soft. Stir in 1 teaspoon tomato paste, then pour over 6 tablespoons dry white wine and bubble for a couple of minutes until reduced by half. Pour in the porcini mushrooms with their soaking liquid and 3 tablespoons sour cream. Fry 5 oz mixed wild mushrooms, trimmed and halved if large, in a little olive oil until soft. While the mushrooms are frying, cook and drain the tagliatelle as above. Toss through the wild mushrooms and mushroom sauce and serve as above.

Conchiglie with Spinach and Goat Cheese

Serves 4

1 tablespoon olive oil
1 garlic clove, finely chopped
5 cups baby spinach leaves, chopped
handful of mint leaves, chopped
1 lb fresh conchiglie
4 oz soft goats' cheese
3 tablespoons roughly chopped walnuts
salt and pepper

- Heat the oil in a large saucepan, add the garlic, and cook for 30 seconds until beginning to turn golden. Add the spinach and cover with a lid. Cook for a couple of minutes or until the spinach has wilted, then stir through the mint.

- Meanwhile, cook the pasta in a large saucepan of salted boiling water according to the package instructions until al dente. Drain, reserving a little cooking water, and return to the pan. Stir through the spinach mixture, adding a little cooking water to loosen, and season with salt and pepper.

- Spoon into serving bowls, crumble over the goat cheese and sprinkle with the walnuts. Serve immediately.

2 Spinach, Zucchini and Olive Conchiglie with Goat Cheese

Cook 14 oz dried conchiglie according to the package instructions until al dente. Meanwhile, cook the garlic, spinach, and mint as above. Slice 14 oz baby zucchini in half. Heat 1 tablespoon olive oil in a skillet, add the zucchini and cook for a couple of minutes. Turn over, add a handful of pitted black olives to the pan, and cook for an additional 2 minutes until golden all over. Drain the pasta, reserving a little of the cooking water, and return to the pan. Toss through the zucchini mixture and spinach, adding a little cooking water to loosen if needed. Serve with goat cheese as above.

3 Spinach, Ham, and Goat Cheese Pasta Bake

Cook 14 oz dried conchiglie according to the package instructions until al dente, adding 5 cups baby spinach leaves just before draining. Meanwhile, melt 2 tablespoons butter in a saucepan and stir in 4 tablespoons all-purpose flour to make a smooth paste. Cook until golden, then gradually whisk in 1¼ cups milk. Bring to a boil and simmer until slightly thickened, stirring often, then stir through 2 oz soft goat cheese. Drain the pasta and spinach and stir into the sauce with 4 slices of ham, cut into bite-size pieces. Pour into an ovenproof dish, crumble over another 2 oz goat cheese and a handful of fresh white bread crumbs. Place in a preheated oven, 400°F, for 15 minutes or until heated through and bubbling.

Fusilli with Lentils, Kale, and Caramelized Onion

Serves 4

2 tablespoons olive oil
2 onions, cut into rings
pinch of dried red pepper flakes
2 garlic cloves, finely sliced
¼ cup Puy lentils, rinsed
  and drained
14 oz tricolore fusilli
1¼ cups chopped kale
salt and pepper

- Heat the oil in a nonstick skillet, add the onions and pepper flakes, season well, and cook over low heat for 15 minutes or until very soft and lightly browned. Add the garlic and cook for an additional couple of minutes.

- Meanwhile, cook the lentils in a saucepan of simmering water according to the package instructions, then drain.

- While the onions and lentils are cooking, cook the pasta in a large saucepan of salted boiling water according to the package instructions until al dente. Add the kale 3 minutes before the end of the cooking time and cook until tender. Drain, reserving a little of the cooking water, and return to the pan. Toss together with the lentils, adding a little cooking water to loosen if needed.

- Spoon into serving bowls and serve sprinkled with the caramelized onions.

Easy Lentil, Caramelized Onion, and Tomato Fusilli

Place an 8 oz pouch ready-cooked Puy lentils in a saucepan and stir in 6 tablespoons store-bought fresh sundried tomato pesto and 2 tablespoons store-bought ready-cooked fried onion. Add 1 chopped tomato and a little water to make a sauce, then heat through. Meanwhile, cook and drain the fusilli as above. Stir through the sauce and serve topped with extra ready-cooked fried onion.

Fusilli with Roasted Shallots and Lentils Place 7 oz peeled shallots in a roasting pan and toss with 2 tablespoons olive oil. Place in a preheated oven, 375°F, for 20–25 minutes or until golden and soft. Drizzle over 1 tablespoon balsamic vinegar and 1 teaspoon sugar and bake for an additional 2 minutes. Meanwhile, cook and drain the lentils and fusilli as above, then toss together with the shallots. Serve drizzled with a little more balsamic vinegar and topped with 1 oz crumbled feta cheese.

Sicilian Cauliflower and Anchovy Rigatoni

Serves 2

7 oz rigatoni
½ small cauliflower, broken
   into florets
1 tablespoon olive oil
4 anchovy fillets in oil, drained
   and finely chopped
2 garlic cloves, sliced
1 red chili, seeded if desired,
   and sliced
3 tablespoons raisins
2½ tablespoons roasted
   pine nuts
juice and grated zest of ½ lemon
salt
chopped flat-leaf parsley,
   to garnish

- Cook the pasta in a large saucepan of salted boiling water according to the package instructions until al dente.

- Meanwhile, cook the cauliflower in a saucepan of boiling water for 5 minutes, then drain. Heat the oil in a small skillet, add the anchovies, garlic, and chili and cook for a couple of minutes until sizzling. Add the cauliflower and cook for an additional couple of minutes until beginning to turn golden. Stir in the raisins and pine nuts, then add the lemon juice.

- Drain the pasta, reserving a little of the cooking water, and return to the pan. Stir through the cauliflower mixture, adding a little cooking water to loosen if needed.

- Spoon into serving bowls and serve sprinkled with the lemon zest and parsley.

Easy Cauliflower Tagliarelle with Anchovy Butter Cook 7 oz tagliarelle according to the package instructions until al dente, adding the cauliflower, prepared as above, for 7 minutes of the cooking time. Meanwhile, mash the grated zest of ½ lemon and 4 drained anchovy fillets into 2 tablespoons softened butter in a bowl. Drain the pasta and cauliflower and spoon into serving bowls. Serve with the anchovy butter dabbed over.

Rigatoni with Roasted Cauliflower in Anchovy Oil Mash together 2 garlic cloves, 5 drained anchovy fillets, and 1 tablespoon oil in a bowl. Place the cauliflower, prepared as above, in a roasting pan and toss in the oil. Place in a preheated oven, 400°F, for 20–25 minutes or until soft and lightly charred. Meanwhile, cook and drain the rigatoni as above. Toss the cauliflower with 1 drained and chopped roasted red pepper from a jar and stir through the pasta with a squeeze of lemon juice. Serve immediately.

30 Spiced Lentils with Angel Hair Pasta

Serves 4

½ cup green or brown lentils, rinsed and drained

3 tablespoons olive oil

3 oz angel hair pasta

1 cup long-grain rice

1¾ cups hot chicken stock

2 large onions, thinly sliced

3 garlic cloves, crushed

¼ teaspoon dried red pepper flakes

1 teaspoon ground cumin

1¾ cups puréed tomatoes

salt and pepper

chopped cilantro leaves, to garnish

- Cook the lentils in a saucepan of simmering water for 25 minutes or according to the package instructions, and drain.

- Meanwhile, heat 1 tablespoon of the oil in a saucepan. Break the pasta into small strips about ¾ inch long. Add to the pan and cook for a couple of minutes until beginning to brown. Add the rice, stir, and then pour over the stock.

- Bring to a boil, then reduce the heat and simmer for about 10 minutes or until the stock has nearly boiled away. Reduce the heat to its lowest setting, cover with a lid, and leave for 5 minutes or until the rice is cooked through.

- While the lentils and rice are cooking, heat the remaining oil in a skillet, add the onions and cook for 20 minutes or until lightly browned, stirring frequently. Add the garlic, pepper flakes and cumin and cook for 1 minute more. Remove some of the onions and set aside. Pour the puréed tomatoes into the pan, season with salt and pepper and simmer until ready.

- Gently stir the lentils through the rice, then spoon into serving bowls. Pour over the spicy tomato sauce and top with the reserved onions, the cilantro and serve.

 Lentil Pasta Salad

Cook 10 oz orzo according to the package instructions. Add ¾ cup frozen fava beans to the pan 3–4 minutes before the end of the cooking time and cook until tender. Drain, then cool under cold running water and drain again. Drain and rinse ¾ cup canned lentils. Mix with the pasta in a dish with 1 finely chopped shallot, the juice of 1 lemon, and a handful of chopped basil leaves.

Lentil Spaghetti Bolognese

Cook 14 oz whole-wheat spaghetti according to the package instructions until al dente. Meanwhile, heat 1 tablespoon olive oil in a large skillet, add 2 sliced garlic cloves, and cook for 1 minute. Pour over 1¾ cups puréed tomatoes and simmer for 10 minutes. Stir in a rinsed and drained 13 oz can lentils and heat through. Drain the pasta and return to the pan.

Mix together with the lentil sauce and serve sprinkled with grated Parmesan cheese, if desired.

Pasta with Zucchini, Peas, Tomatoes, and Feta

Serves 4

2 zucchini
1 tablespoon olive oil
14 oz tagliarelle pasta
⅔ cup frozen peas
2 oz feta cheese
½ cup cherry tomatoes, halved
salt and pepper
basil leaves, to garnish

- Using a vegetable peeler, thinly slice the zucchini, then rub over the oil and season well with salt and pepper. Heat a griddle pan until smoking, then add the zucchini and cook for about 2 minutes. Turn over and cook for an additional 2 minutes until just soft and lightly charred. Set aside.

- Cook the pasta in a large saucepan of salted boiling water according to the package instructions until al dente. Add the peas 2 minutes before the end of the cooking time and cook until tender. Drain, reserving a little of the cooking water, and return to the pan.

- Mash half the feta with 2 tablespoons of the cooking water and stir through the pasta, adding more cooking water to loosen if needed. Toss together with the tomatoes and zucchini. Crumble over the remaining feta and serve sprinkled with basil leaves.

 Quick Zucchini, Pea, Tomato, and Feta Pasta Cook the tagliarelle pasta and peas as above. Meanwhile, mash together 2 oz feta cheese, 2 tablespoons milk, a handful of chopped mint leaves, and 4 drained and finely chopped sundried tomatoes in oil in a bowl, then finely grate in 2 zucchini. Drain the pasta and peas, then toss through the zucchini mixture. Serve immediately.

Zucchini, Tomato, and Feta Pasta Bake with Pea Shoots Cook 14 oz fusilli according to package instructions until al dente. Drain and return to the pan, then mix through a 13 oz can chopped tomatoes. Meanwhile, cook the zucchini as above and then stir into the pasta with a handful of chopped basil leaves. Pour into an ovenproof dish, sprinkle over a handful of dried white bread crumbs and 3 oz crumbled feta cheese. Place in a preheated oven, 375°F, for 15 minutes or until golden and cooked through. Serve topped with pea shoot leaves mixed with a little lemon juice and extra virgin olive oil.

PAS-HEAL-MUG

Spaghetti with Mini Tuna Balls

Serves 4

2 scallions, thinly sliced

2 x 6½ oz cans tuna in spring
water, drained

1 egg yolk, lightly beaten

1 cup fresh white bread crumbs

handful of mint leaves, chopped,
plus extra to garnish (optional)

pinch of dried red pepper flakes

1 tablespoon olive oil

1½ cups store-bought tomato
pasta sauce

14 oz spaghetti

salt and pepper

- Mix together the scallions, tuna, egg yolk, bread crumbs, mint, and pepper flakes in a bowl and season with salt and pepper. Lightly wet your hands, then shape the mixture into small balls, each about the size of a walnut. The mixture should make about 12 balls.

- Heat the oil in a nonstick skillet and cook the tuna balls for 5–10 minutes or until golden all over and cooked through. Pour over the tomato pasta sauce and cook for an additional 5 minutes until the sauce is heated through, adding a little extra water if the sauce becomes too thick.

- Meanwhile, cook the pasta in a large saucepan of salted boiling water according to the package instructions until al dente. Drain and stir through the sauce.

- Spoon into serving bowls and serve sprinkled with extra chopped mint, if desired.

Simple Tuna Spaghetti Cook and drain the spaghetti as above. Meanwhile, toss together a drained 4 oz can tuna in spring water, 1 chopped red chili, seeded if desired, 10 halved cherry tomatoes and a good squeeze of lemon juice in a bowl. Stir through the drained pasta with a large handful of arugula leaves. Serve immediately.

Spaghetti with Spiced Fresh Tuna Balls Chop a 14 oz piece of fresh tuna on a cutting board as finely as you can. Make the mini tuna balls as above, replacing the canned tuna with the fresh tuna and adding 1 teaspoon ground cumin and 1½ tablespoons raisins. Continue with the recipe as above.

Pasta Primavera

Serves 4

14 oz farfalle
1 tablespoon olive oil
4 scallions, sliced
2 tablespoons dry white wine
5 oz asparagus tips
⅔ cup frozen fava beans
3 tablespoons low-fat cream
  cheese
salt and pepper
chopped chives, to garnish

- Cook the pasta in a large saucepan of salted boiling water according to the package instructions until al dente.

- Meanwhile, heat the oil in a skillet with a lid, add the scallions and cook for 1–2 minutes until softened. Pour over the wine and bubble for a couple of minutes until syrupy. Add the asparagus and 3 tablespoons water, then cover with the lid and simmer for 5 minutes.

- Add the fava beans to the pan, followed by the cream cheese. Stir around, adding more water if needed until the cream cheese melts into the sauce and the fava beans are tender.

- Drain the pasta, reserving a little of the cooking water, and return to the pan. Stir through the vegetable sauce, adding a little cooking water to loosen if needed.

- Spoon into serving bowls and serve sprinkled with chives.

 Speedy Pasta Primavera Cook 14 oz spaghettini according to package instructions until al dente. Add the asparagus and fava beans to the pan 3 minutes before the end of the cooking time and cook until tender. Meanwhile, mix together the cream cheese with 2–3 table-spoons store-bought fresh green pesto in a bowl. Drain the pasta and vegetables, reserving a little of the cooking water, and return to the pan. Stir the cream cheese mixture into the pasta, adding a little cooking water to loosen, and serve immediately.

 Pasta Primavera with Griddled Vegetables Heat a griddle pan until smoking hot. Toss 4 sliced scallions, 5 oz asparagus tips and 4 oz trimmed and cleaned baby leeks with olive oil in a bowl, then place half the vegetables in the hot griddle pan and cook for 7–10 minutes or until soft and charred. Remove from the pan and keep warm, then repeat with the remaining vegetables. Meanwhile, cook and drain the farfalle as above. Toss through the griddled vegetables with a good squeeze of lemon juice, a little cooking water, and a big handful of grated Parmesan cheese. Chop together the zest of ½ lemon, 1 garlic clove, and 1 tablespoon flat-leaf parsley. Serve sprinkled over the pasta.

3 Penne with Caponata Sauce

Serves 4

1 eggplant, cubed
4 tablespoons olive oil
1 onion, sliced
1 garlic clove, sliced
2 celery sticks, sliced
½ cup large pitted
  green olives
1 tablespoon capers, rinsed
  and drained
3 tablespoons white wine vinegar
2 tablespoons sugar
13 oz can cherry tomatoes
14 oz penne
salt and pepper
torn basil leaves, to garnish

- Toss the eggplant in 2 tablespoons of the oil, place on a baking sheet, and season with salt and pepper. Place in a preheated oven, 375°F, for 20 minutes until soft and browned.

- Meanwhile, make the caponata sauce. Heat the remaining oil in a large skillet, add the onion and garlic, and cook gently for 5 minutes. Add the celery and cook for an additional 5 minutes until very soft. Stir in the olives and capers, followed by the vinegar, sugar, and tomatoes. Bring to a boil, then reduce the heat and simmer for 15 minutes, adding the baked eggplant to heat through for a couple of minutes. Season to taste.

- While the eggplant and sauce are cooking, cook the pasta in a large saucepan of salted boiling water according to the package instructions until al dente. Drain, reserving a little of the cooking water, and return to the pan. Toss through the sauce, adding a little cooking water to loosen if needed.

- Spoon into serving bowls and serve sprinkled with the basil.

 Quick Eggplant and Tomato Pasta

Cut 1 eggplant into thin slices, rub with olive oil, and season well. Cook under a preheated hot broiler for 3–5 minutes on each side. Meanwhile, cook the penne as above. Mix together 1 tablespoon balsamic vinegar, ½ teaspoon sugar, and 3 tablespoons extra virgin olive oil in a bowl and season. Drain the pasta and return to the pan. Mix together with the eggplant, 10 halved cherry tomatoes, and the dressing. Serve immediately.

 Penne with Eggplant Caponata Sauce Make the caponata sauce as above, omitting the celery. Meanwhile, rub oil onto thin slices of eggplant, season, and cook under a preheated hot broiler for 3 minutes on each side. Add to the sauce with 2 teaspoons grated bittersweet chocolate to enrich the sauce and heat through. While the sauce is cooking, cook and drain the penne as above. Stir through the sauce and serve immediately.

Roast Chicken, Tomato, and Feta Pasta

Serves 4

2 tablespoons olive oil
2 boneless, skinless
　chicken breasts
1 teaspoon honey
juice of 1 lemon
¾ cup cherry tomatoes
14 oz ruote pasta
handful of oregano leaves,
　chopped
1 oz feta cheese
salt and pepper

- Brush a little of the oil over each chicken breast, then place on a baking sheet and season well with salt and pepper. Place in a preheated oven, 400°F, for 12 minutes or until nearly cooked through.

- Drizzle over the honey and a good squeeze of the lemon juice and spread the tomatoes around. Return to the oven and cook for an additional 5 minutes or until the chicken is cooked through.

- Meanwhile, cook the pasta in a large saucepan of salted boiling water according to the package instructions until al dente. Drain, reserving a little of the cooking water, and return to the pan. Stir through lemon juice to taste, the remaining oil, and the oregano.

- Cut the chicken into bite-size pieces and stir through the pasta with the tomatoes, adding a little cooking water if needed. Spoon into serving bowls, crumble over the feta cheese, and serve immediately.

 Simple Chicken, Tomato, and Feta Tagliarelle Cook and drain 14 oz tagliarelle according to the package instructions until al dente. Toss through 2 store-bought roasted chicken breasts, skin discarded and flesh torn into shreds, a large handful of drained sunblush tomatoes in oil, and a little balsamic vinegar to taste. Serve sprinkled with basil leaves and the feta as above.

 Tomato and Feta Pasta with Griddled Chicken Mix together 1 crushed garlic clove, a handful of oregano leaves, the juice of ½ lemon, and 3 tablespoons extra virgin olive oil in a bowl, then add 2 boneless, skinless chicken breasts and marinate for 15 minutes. Heat a griddle pan until smoking, then add the chicken and cook for 5–7 minutes on each side or until just cooked through. Drizzle a little olive oil over ¾ cup cherry tomatoes on a baking sheet and cook under a preheated hot broiler for 1–2 minutes until lightly coloured. Meanwhile, cook and drain the ruote pasta as above. Mash 2 oz feta cheese with 3 tablespoons sour cream in a bowl and toss through the drained pasta with the tomatoes. Cut the chicken into slices and serve on top of the pasta with extra feta crumbled over, if desired.

# Red Pepper and Walnut Spaghetti

Serves 4

2 tablespoons olive oil
2 bell peppers
1 shallot, finely chopped
1 garlic clove, finely chopped
¾ cup walnuts
1 tablespoon pomegranate
  molasses or balsamic vinegar
  to taste
4 tablespoons low-fat cream
  cheese
14 oz spaghetti
handful of chopped flat-leaf
  parsley
salt and pepper

- Rub 1 tablespoon of the olive oil over the red peppers. Cook under a preheated hot broiler for 10 minutes, turning frequently, until charred all over. Place in a plastic food bag, seal, and leave for 5 minutes. When cool, peel away the blackened skin. Cut in half, remove the seeds, and slice.

- Meanwhile, heat the remaining oil in a small skillet, add the shallot and garlic, and cook for 3–5 minutes until softened. Dry-fry the walnuts in a separate skillet, shaking frequently, for 3 minutes or until lightly toasted. Add the shallot mixture and most of the walnuts, reserving a few, to a food processor or blender with the pomegranate molasses or balsamic vinegar and whiz together to form a thick paste. Stir in the cream cheese and season with salt and pepper.

- Cook the pasta in a large pan of salted boiling water according to package instructions until al dente. Drain, reserving a couple of tablespoons of the cooking water, and return to the pan. Toss through the nut paste, adding cooking water to loosen. Stir in the peppers and parsley. Pile in serving bowls and serve sprinkled with the reserved nuts.

 Spaghetti with Quick Red Pepper and Walnut Sauce Cook and drain the spaghetti as above. Meanwhile, place the walnuts, garlic, and cream cheese as above with 2 drained roasted red peppers from a jar and a handful of chopped basil leaves in a small food processor or blender and whiz together to form a sauce. Toss through the drained pasta and serve topped with extra chopped walnuts, if desired.

 Red Pepper and Walnut Spaghetti with Mussels Grill and skin the red peppers as above, then finely chop. Meanwhile, heat a little olive oil in a large saucepan, add 1 chopped shallot and 2 chopped garlic cloves, and cook until softened. Pour over 6 table-spoons dry white wine and 100 ml 6 tablespoons hot fish stock and cook for 10 minutes until reduced down. Add 1 lb debearded and cleaned mussels, cover with a lid, and cook for 5 minutes until the mussels have opened. Discard any that remain closed. Remove the mussels from the pan. While the peppers and sauce are cooking, cook and drain the spaghetti as above. Chop ¾ cup walnuts and add to the pan with 4 tablespoons low-fat cream cheese and the red peppers. Stir to make a sauce, then return the mussels to the pan with the drained pasta and toss together. Serve sprinkled with chopped flat-leaf parsley.

Pasta with Seafood and Roasted Butternut Squash

Serves 4

13 oz butternut squash, peeled, seeded, and cubed

2 tablespoons olive oil

14 oz tripoline pasta

1 onion, finely chopped

2 garlic cloves, finely chopped

1 red chili, seeded if desired, and finely chopped

5 tablespoons dry white wine

1 lb mussels, debearded and cleaned

salt and pepper

chopped cilantro leaves, to garnish

- Toss the butternut squash in 1 tablespoon of the oil in a roasting pan and season well with salt and pepper. Place in a preheated oven, 400°F, for 15 minutes. Turn over and cook for an additional 10 minutes or until soft and lightly browned.

- Meanwhile, cook the pasta in a large saucepan of salted boiling water according to the package instructions until al dente.

- Heat the remaining oil in another large saucepan, add the onion, garlic, and chili and cook for a couple of minutes until softened. Pour over the wine and bring to a boil. Reduce the heat and simmer for 1–2 minutes. Add the mussels, cover with a lid, and cook for 5 minutes until the mussels have opened. Discard any that remain closed.

- Drain the pasta and return to the pan. Stir in the butternut squash and mussels with all the cooking juices. Season well.

- Spoon into serving bowls and serve sprinkled with the cilantro.

---

1 **Easy Butternut Squash and Seafood Tripoline** Cook 14 oz penne and the butternut squash, prepared as above, in a large saucepan of boiling water for 10 minutes until soft. Drain, return to the pan, and toss together with 7 oz store-bought ready-cooked mussels, a good squeeze of lemon juice, red pepper, and some dried red pepper flakes. Serve as above.

 2 **Pasta with Butternut Squash and Seafood Sauce** Heat a little olive oil in a large skillet, add the butternut squash, prepared as above, and cook over low heat for 12–15 minutes or until soft. Place in a food processor or blender and whiz to form a purée. Heat a little olive oil in a skillet, add 1 finely chopped onion, and cook, until softened, then add the squash,

5 tablespoons half-fat sour cream and enough water to make a sauce. Add 7 oz large cooked peeled shrimp and cook for 3 minutes or until heated through. Meanwhile, cook and drain the tripoline pasta as above. Stir through the sauce and serve sprinkled with 1 oz soft goat cheese and chopped flat-leaf parsley.

Gnocchi with Salmon in a Chili Tomato Sauce

Serves 4

2 tablespoons olive oil
8 oz piece of salmon fillet
1 onion, finely chopped
2 garlic cloves, finely chopped
1 teaspoon tomato paste
1–2 tablespoons sweet chili sauce
13 oz can chopped tomatoes
14 oz dried gnocchi pasta
salt and pepper
basil leaves, to garnish

- Rub 1 tablespoon of the olive oil over the salmon and season well with salt and pepper. Place on a baking sheet and cook in a preheated oven, 375°F, for 12–15 minutes or until the fish is cooked through and flakes easily.

- Meanwhile, heat the remaining oil in a saucepan, add the onion and garlic, and cook for a couple of minutes until softened. Stir in the tomato paste, then add the sweet chili sauce and tomatoes. Bring to a boil, then reduce the heat and simmer until ready to serve.

- Cook the pasta in a large saucepan of salted boiling water according to the package instructions until al dente. Drain, reserving a little of the cooking water, and return to the pan. Stir through the tomato sauce, adding a little cooking water if needed. Carefully flake the fish, removing any skin and bones, and add to the pasta.

- Spoon into serving bowls and serve sprinkled with basil leaves.

 Quick Gnocchi with Chili Tomatoes and Salmon Cook and drain the gnocchi as above. Meanwhile, mix together ¾ cup halved cherry tomatoes, 3 tablespoons sweet chili sauce and a handful of chopped basil leaves in a bowl. Stir into the drained pasta with 2 hot-smoked salmon fillets torn into bite-size pieces. Serve immediately.

 Salmon, Tomato and Chili Pasta Salad Cook 10 oz ditalini according to the package instructions. Drain, then cool under cold running water and drain again. Meanwhile, place an 8 oz piece of salmon fillet in a skillet and pour over enough dry white wine and fish stock to cover, then poach for 15 minutes or until just cooked through. Remove any skin and bones,

then flake. Mix together a good squeeze of lemon juice, 1 teaspoon honey, 1 seeded and chopped chili and 3 tablespoons extra virgin olive oil in a bowl. Chop and seed 3 ripe tomatoes. Using a vegetable peeler, slice ½ cucumber into thin curls. Toss everything together in a large serving dish and serve sprinkled with chopped cilantro leaves.

PAS-HEAL-KEI

Summer Vegetable Tortiglioni with Basil Vinaigrette

Serves 4

2 tablespoons olive oil

1 red bell pepper, cored, seeded and sliced

1 eggplant, sliced

1 zucchini, sliced

10 baby plum tomatoes, halved

14 oz tortiglioni

3 tablespoons toasted pine nuts, to serve

For the basil vinaigrette

1 tablespoon white wine vinegar

½ teaspoon Dijon mustard

2 tablespoons extra virgin olive oil

large handful of basil leaves, finely chopped

salt and pepper

- Rub the olive oil over the red pepper, eggplant, zucchini and tomatoes and season well with salt and pepper. Heat a griddle pan until smoking, then add the vegetables and cook in batches until softened and lightly charred.

- Meanwhile, cook the pasta in a large saucepan of salted boiling water according to the package instructions until al dente. Drain the pasta, reserving a little of the cooking water.

- To make the vinaigrette, whisk together the vinegar and mustard in a small bowl. Slowly drizzle in the oil, whisking all the time, until a smooth vinaigrette forms. Season and stir in the basil. Alternatively, make the vinaigrette in a small food processor or blender.

- Return the pasta to the pan. Stir through a little of the vinaigrette and the griddled vegetables, adding a little cooking water to loosen if needed.

- Spoon into serving bowls and drizzle over the remaining vinaigrette. Serve sprinkled with the pine nuts.

Easy Grilled Vegetable Penne

Cook and drain 14 oz penne according to the package instructions until al dente. Meanwhile, mix together 2 oz soft goat cheese and 3 tablespoons store-bought fresh green pesto in a bowl. Toss 1 chopped ready-grilled eggplant, and 1 chopped ready-grilled pepper, and the cheese mixture through the drained pasta. Serve immediately.

 Tortiglioni with Ratatouille Sauce

Chop the vegetables into small pieces. Heat a little olive oil in a skillet, add the vegetables and cook in batches until golden. Meanwhile, heat 2 tablespoons olive oil in a separate saucepan, add 1 finely chopped onion and 1 finely chopped garlic clove and cook until softened. Pour over 6 tablespoons dry white wine and cook for 5 minutes, then pour over a 13 oz can chopped tomatoes and simmer for an additional 10 minutes. Remove the pan from the heat and whiz together with an immersion blender and then add the vegetables. Return to the heat and simmer for an additional 10 minutes, season well, and add a handful of chopped basil leaves. While the vegetable sauce is cooking, cook and drain the tortiglioni as above. Toss the vegetable sauce through the pasta and serve immediately.

Fennel, Olive, and Orange Pappardelle

Serves 4

2 tablespoons olive oil
1 fennel bulb, thinly sliced
1 red onion, sliced
2 garlic cloves, sliced
1 orange
5 tablespoons dry white wine
⅓ cup pitted black olives
14 oz pappardelle
salt
chopped basil leaves, to garnish

- Heat the oil in a medium saucepan, add the fennel, onion, and garlic and cook over low heat for 10 minutes until softened. Using a sharp knife, peel off a strip of orange peel and add to the pan with the wine. Bring to a boil, then reduce the heat and add the olives. Simmer for about 10 minutes, adding a little water if needed.

- Meanwhile, cook the pasta in a large saucepan of salted boiling water according to the package instructions until al dente. Drain, reserving a little of the cooking water. Toss through the sauce (removing the orange peel), adding a little cooking water to loosen if needed.

- Spoon into serving bowls and finely grate over a little orange zest. Serve sprinkled with the basil.

 Quick Fennel, Olive, and Orange Pappardelle Cook the pappardelle as above. Meanwhile, heat a little olive oil in a skillet, add 1 finely chopped fennel bulb and 1 chopped garlic clove, and cook for 3 minutes until golden. Pour over 3 tablespoons vermouth and let bubble away, then squeeze in the juice of ½ orange. Drain the pasta and return to the pan, then toss through ⅓ cup pitted black olives, a handful of chopped basil leaves, and the fennel sauce.

Grilled Swordfish with Fennel, Olive, and Orange Pasta Salad Cut 1 fennel bulb into thick strips. Brush with olive oil, then cook under a preheated hot broiler for 3 minutes on each side or until lightly charred. Set aside to cool. Cook 14 oz penne according to the package instructions. Drain, then cool under cold running water and drain again. Brush olive oil over 4 swordfish steaks, season with salt and pepper, and cook under a preheated medium broiler for 5–7 minutes on each side or until just cooked through. Toss together the cooled pasta, fennel, ⅓ cup pitted black olives, 5 chopped tomatoes, 2 tablespoons extra virgin olive oil and a little grated orange zest. Serve alongside the swordfish steaks.

30 Penne with Blackened Broccoli, Chili and Garlic

Serves 4

1 head of broccoli
3 tablespoons olive oil
4 garlic cloves, thinly sliced
1 red chili, seeded if desired,
  and sliced
14 oz whole-wheat penne
juice and grated zest of ½ lemon
salt and pepper

- Cut the broccoli into bite-size florets, then place on a baking sheet and drizzle over 2 tablespoons of the oil and season well with salt and pepper. Place in a preheated oven, 375°F, for 20 minutes or until soft and beginning to char all over.

- Add the garlic and chili, return to the oven and cook for an additional 2 minutes until they are lightly browned.

- Meanwhile, cook the pasta in a large saucepan of salted boiling water according to the package instructions until al dente. Drain and return to the pan. Stir in the grated lemon zest and add lemon juice to taste.

- Tip in the cooked broccoli, garlic, and chili, then season. Stir through the remaining oil and serve immediately.

 Penne and Broccoli with Chili and Garlic Oil Cook the penne as above. Add 1 head of broccoli, broken into florets, to the pan 4–5 minutes before the end of the cooking time and cook until just tender. Meanwhile, heat 3 tablespoons olive oil in a skillet, add the chili, garlic, and grated lemon zest as above and cook for 1–2 minutes. Drain the pasta and broccoli and return to the pan. Toss through the flavored oil and a squeeze of lemon juice and serve immediately.

 Penne with Griddled Garlic and Chili Broccoli Cook and drain the penne as above. Meanwhile, cook 1 head of broccoli, broken into florets, in a saucepan of boiling water for 2 minutes. Drain well and pat dry with paper towels, then toss with 1 tablespoon olive oil, 1 crushed garlic clove, and a pinch of dried red pepper flakes. Heat a griddle pan, add the broccoli, and cook for a couple of minutes until lightly browned all over. Toss together with the drained pasta and a squeeze of lemon juice. Serve immediately.

Sin-Free Macaroni and Cheese with Tomato

Serves 4

14 oz elbow macaroni
2 tablespoons cornstarch
2 cups milk
8 oz silken tofu
1 ½ cups grated Cheddar
cheese
2 tablespoons grated Parmesan
cheese
1 large tomato, sliced
salt and pepper

- Cook the pasta in a large saucepan of salted boiling water according to the package instructions until al dente.

- Meanwhile, place the cornstarch in a small saucepan and whisk in 4 tablespoons of the milk until smooth. Gradually add the remaining milk, then bring to a boil and simmer until slightly thickened.

- Place the tofu in a food processor or blender and whiz until a smooth paste forms. Add in the milk mixture and process until smooth. Stir in most of the cheeses and season well with salt and pepper.

- Drain the pasta, then stir through the tofu sauce. Spoon into an ovenproof dish and sprinkle with the remaining cheese, then arrange the tomato on top.

- Place in a preheated oven, 375°F, for 15 minutes or until golden, crispy on top, and cooked through.

 Simple Cream Cheese and Tomato Pasta Cook and drain 14 oz chifferi pasta according to the package instructions, reserving a little of the cooking water. Meanwhile, mix together 6 tablespoons low-fat cream cheese and a large handful of grated Parmesan cheese in a bowl. Stir through the drained pasta, adding a little cooking water to loosen if needed, and serve sprinkled with 2 ripe chopped tomatoes.

 Macaroni and Cheese and Tomato Gratin Cook and drain the macaroni as above. Meanwhile, make the tofu sauce as above. Stir the sauce through the pasta with 5 drained and chopped sunblush tomatoes in oil and a handful of basil leaves. Spoon into a heatproof dish, top with a handful of fresh white bread crumbs, and a little extra Parmesan, if desired, and cook under a preheated hot broiler for a couple of minutes until lightly browned.

QuickCook
Food for Friends

Recipes listed by cooking time

30

20

10

Light Clam and Tomato Broth

Serves 4

5 oz tomatoes
2 tablespoons olive oil
2 garlic cloves, finely chopped
⅔ cup dry white wine
8 cups hot chicken or fish stock
5 sundried tomatoes in oil,
   drained and finely chopped
7 oz anellini pasta
2 lb clams, cleaned
salt and pepper
chopped flat-leaf parsley,
   to garnish
lemon wedges and
crusty bread, to serve

- Cut a cross at the stem end of each tomato, place in a heatproof bowl, and pour over boiling water to cover. Leave for 1–2 minutes, then drain and peel off the skins. Halve the tomatoes, remove the seeds, and roughly chop.

- Heat the oil in a large saucepan, add the garlic, and cook for 30 seconds until beginning to turn golden. Pour over the wine and cook for 5 minutes until slightly reduced. Pour over the stock and bring to a boil. Add the fresh and sundried tomatoes, season with salt and pepper, and simmer for 5 minutes.

- Add the pasta and clams, cover with a lid, and cook for 5 minutes until the pasta has cooked through and the clams have opened. Discard any that remain closed. Season to taste.

- Ladle into serving bowls, sprinkle with the parsley, and serve with the lemon wedges and crusty bread.

Simple Spaghetti with Clams Heat a little olive oil in a large saucepan, add 1 finely chopped garlic clove and 1 chopped red chili and cook for 1 minute until softened. Pour over 5 tablespoons dry white wine and add the cleaned clams as above. Cover and cook for 5 minutes until the clams have opened. Discard any that stay closed. Meanwhile, cook 14 oz spaghetti according to the package instructions until al dente. Drain and return to the pan. Toss through the clams and their cooking liquid, 3 tablespoons sour cream and a handful of chopped flat-leaf parsley.

Linguine with Barbecued Clams Heat a little olive oil in a skillet, add 1 finely sliced shallot and 1 chopped red chili, seeded if desired, and cook for a couple of minutes until softened. Pour over 5 tablespoons dry white wine and a pinch of saffron threads. Simmer for 5 minutes until reduced down. Pour over ¾ cup store-bought clam juice and simmer for a further 10 minutes until reduced down. Place the cleaned clams as above on the grill rack of a barbecue. Cook for 5–7 minutes, transfer to a baking sheet as they open, and top with a little garlic butter.

Discard any clams that remain closed. Cook for an additional 5 minutes on the barbecue until the butter starts to melt. Meanwhile, cook 14 oz linguine according to the package instructions until al dente. Drain and toss through the sauce. Serve topped with the grilled clams.

30 Linguine with Tuna Sashimi and Arugula

Serves 2

5 oz very fresh tuna steak
7 oz linguine
3 tablespoons extra virgin olive oil, plus extra to serve
juice of ½ lemon
1¼ cups arugula leaves
salt and pepper
Parmesan cheese shavings, to serve

- Wrap the tuna tightly in plastic wrap and place in a freezer for 20 minutes and then, using a sharp knife, slice into very thin strips.

- Meanwhile, cook the pasta in a large saucepan of salted boiling water according to the package instructions until al dente. Drain the pasta and return to the pan, then toss through the tuna with 1 tablespoon olive oil and lemon juice.

- Toss together the arugula and remaining lemon juice and 1 tablespoon oil in a bowl and season with salt and pepper.

- Spoon the pasta into serving bowls, arrange the arugula salad on top, and grind over plenty of black pepper. Serve sprinkled with the Parmesan shavings and drizzled with the remaining olive oil.

 Wintery Tuna and Arugula Linguine
Cook the linguine as above. Meanwhile, mix together 1 egg yolk, the juice and grated zest of 1 lemon, and 1 crushed garlic clove in a bowl. Drain the pasta and return to the pan. Stir through the egg mixture, 5½ oz canned tuna, drained and flaked, a handful of rinsed and drained capers, and 1¼ cups arugula leaves. Serve immediately.

 Linguine with Griddled Tuna and Arugula Cook and drain the linguine as above. Meanwhile, rub a little olive oil over 1 large tuna steak and season well with salt and plenty of pepper. Heat a griddle pan until smoking, add the tuna and cook for 3–5 minutes on each side or until browned on the outside but still rare inside, then leave to rest for a few minutes before cutting into thick slices. Toss 1¼ cups arugula leaves in a little lemon juice and olive oil. Stir the tuna slices and arugula through the drained pasta and serve topped with Parmesan cheese shavings.

Zingy Crab Angel Hair Pasta

Serves 4

14 oz angel hair pasta
8 oz fresh white crabmeat
6 tablespoons sour cream
juice and grated zest of ½ lemon
1 red chili, seeded and
    finely chopped
handful of flat-leaf parsley,
    chopped
salt and pepper

- Cook the pasta in a large saucepan of salted boiling water according to the package instructions until al dente. Drain, reserving a little of the cooking water, and return to the pan.

- Stir through the remaining ingredients, adding a little cooking water to loosen if needed, and season well with salt and pepper. Serve immediately.

Crab and Prosciutto Angel Hair Pasta

Heat a little olive oil in a skillet, add 1 finely chopped shallot, and cook over a low heat until softened. Add 1 sliced garlic clove and cook for 1 minute more, then add 5 oz diced prosciutto and cook over medium heat for a couple of minutes until golden. Pour over 6 tablespoons dry white wine and cook until reduced. Stir through the sour cream and crabmeat as above and heat through. Meanwhile, cook and drain the angel hair pasta as above, then stir through the sauce. Serve immediately.

Pasta with Fresh Crab

Cook the crab in 8 cups vegetable stock and ⅔ cup dry white wine for 7 minutes per lb. Once the crab has boiled, remove from the water and allow it to cool while cooking your pasta. Cook 14 oz angel hair pasta according to the pack instructions until al dente. Pull off the claws and legs and then, with the crab's body on its back and facing away from you, bring your thumbs up under the rear edge and push firmly to lift out the core. Dig your thumb in behind the eyes and mouthparts and lift out the mass of bony and gloopy bits – the inedible parts of the digestive tract. Remove, crack open the shell, and dig out the meat inside. Meanwhile, heat a little butter in a skillet, add 1 shallot and cook until softened.

Stir in 2 tablespoons of the brown crabmeat, then pour over 3 tablespoons dry white wine (or the reduced poaching liquid). Simmer for a couple of minutes, then add the sour cream and white crabmeat as above. Drain the pasta and return to the pan. Stir through the crab sauce and serve immediately.

Pasta with Rich Mushroom Sauce and Prosciutto

Serves 6

2 tablespoons butter
1 tablespoon olive oil
1 shallot, finely chopped
1 small garlic clove, crushed
5 tablespoons dry white wine
3 tablespoons hot chicken stock
½ cup heavy cream
¼ cup grated Parmesan cheese,
    plus extra to serve (optional)
6 slices of prosciutto
14 oz mixed wild mushrooms,
    trimmed and halved if large
1¼ lb riccioli al barolo pasta
fresh basil, to garnish
salt and pepper

- Heat half of the butter and half the oil in a saucepan, add the shallot and garlic, and cook for a couple of minutes until softened. Pour over the wine and bubble vigorously until syrupy and reduced down to a couple of tablespoons of liquid. Pour over the stock and cook for an additional 5 minutes, then stir in the cream and Parmesan, season with salt and pepper and keep warm.

- Heat the remaining butter and oil in a skillet, add the prosciutto slices, and cook for 1–2 minutes until they start to sizzle. Remove from the pan and set aside. Add the mushrooms to the pan and fry for 3–5 minutes or until golden and cooked through. Stir into the sauce.

- Meanwhile, cook the pasta in a large saucepan of salted boiling water according to the package instructions until al dente. Drain the pasta, reserving a little of the cooking water. Toss through the mushroom sauce, adding a little cooking water if needed.

- Spoon into serving bowls, crumble over the prosciutto, and serve sprinkled with extra Parmesan if desired and basil.

Mushroom and Pesto Pasta

Cook 1¼ lb pasta as above. Meanwhile, fry the mushrooms as above in a little olive oil until softened. Drain the pasta and return to the pan. Stir through the mushrooms and 6 table-spoons store-bought fresh green pesto. Serve topped with a handful of toasted pine nuts.

Mushroom Pasta with Slow-Cooked

Leeks Heat a little olive oil in a skillet, add 5 oz pancetta cubes and cook over high heat for 5 minutes or until crispy. Reduce the heat and add 4 trimmed, cleaned, and sliced leeks, 1 tablespoon chopped thyme leaves, and a splash of water and cook gently for 15 minutes or until very soft and lightly caramelized. Stir through

5 tablespoons heavy cream and 4 oz Taleggio cheese, cubed, to make a sauce. Drizzle olive oil over the mushrooms, prepared as above, in a broiler and cook under a preheated hot broiler for 5 minutes or until lightly charred. Meanwhile, cook and drain the riccioli al barolo as above. Stir through the mushrooms and leek sauce and serve immediately.

Creamy Vodka and Tomato Tacconelli

Serves 4

1 tablespoon butter
8 pancetta slices
1 rosemary sprig
5 tablespoons vodka
1½ cups store-bought tomato pasta sauce
14 oz tacconelli
⅔ cup heavy cream
salt and pepper
grated Parmesan cheese, to serve

- Heat the butter in a saucepan, add the pancetta, and cook for about 3 minutes until golden and crispy. Remove from the pan and keep warm. Stir in the rosemary, then remove from the heat and pour over the vodka. Return to high heat and cook until the vodka has reduced down to 1 tablespoon. Pour over the tomato pasta sauce, reduce the heat, and simmer for 10 minutes.

- Meanwhile, cook the pasta in a large saucepan of salted boiling water according to the package instructions until al dente.

- Remove the rosemary from the sauce, then stir in the cream. Drain the pasta, reserving a little of the cooking water, and return to the pan. Stir through the sauce, adding a little cooking water to loosen if needed, and season with salt and pepper.

- Spoon into serving bowls, top with the pancetta slices, and serve sprinkled with the Parmesan.

 Quick Vodka and Tomato Penne
Cook 1 lb fresh penne as above. Meanwhile, heat a little olive oil in a skillet, add 3 tablespoons tomato paste, and cook for 30 seconds. Add ½ cup halved baby plum tomatoes and 2 tablespoons vodka and cook for a couple of minutes until the tomatoes have softened, then stir in ⅔ cup heavy cream. Drain the pasta and return to the pan. Toss through the sauce and serve immediately.

 Vodka Penne with Slow-Roasted Tomatoes Place 10 halved baby plum tomatoes in a roasting pan, drizzle over a little olive oil, and season. Place in a preheated oven, 300°F, for 20–25 minutes until lightly browned. Meanwhile, cook the penne as above. Heat 3 tablespoons vodka in a small saucepan and bubble until reduced down to 1 tablespoon. Pour over 5 tablespoons heavy cream and stir through ¼ cup grated Parmesan cheese. Drain the pasta and return to the pan. Toss through the sauce, roasted tomatoes, and a handful of chopped basil leaves. Serve immediately.

Salmon and Zucchini Pasta

Serves 4

⅔ cup dry white wine
⅔ cup sour cream
a squeeze of lemon juice
handful of dill weed, chopped
12 lasagna sheets
2 zucchini
4 hot-smoked salmon fillets
3 scallions, sliced
salt and pepper

- Bring the wine to a boil in a small saucepan and boil for 5 minutes until syrupy and reduced by half. Add the sour cream, a squeeze of lemon juice, and most of the dill. Season with salt and pepper, then stir until mixed through.

- Meanwhile, cook the lasagna sheets in a large saucepan of salted boiling water for 3–5 minutes or until soft, then drain well. Shave the zucchini into long thin strips using a vegetable peeler.

- Cut each lasagna sheet into large irregular shapes and place in a bowl. Break the salmon into large chunks.

- Arrange the salmon and pasta on serving plates with the zucchini ribbons. Drizzle over the sauce and serve sprinkled with the scallions and the remaining dill.

10 **Summery Zucchini, Asparagus, and Salmon Fettuccine** Cook 14 oz fettuccine according to the package instructions until al dente. Add 7 oz asparagus tips to the pan 3 minutes before the end of the cooking time and cook until just tender. Drain and return to the pan. Toss through 2 hot-smoked salmon fillets, flaked into pieces, the grated zest of 1 lemon, and 6 table-spoons sour cream. Serve topped with 1 zucchini, cut into ribbons as above.

30 **Zucchini and Salmon Lasagna** Prepare 12 fresh lasagna sheets, if necessary, according to the package instructions. Make the wine sauce as above, then grate 2 zucchini and stir into the sauce with the flaked salmon fillets. Layer up the sauce and lasagna sheets in an ovenproof dish, finishing with a layer of lasagna. Mix together ¾ cup sour cream and 4 oz ricotta cheese in a bowl and thin with milk to make a sauce. Pour over the lasagna, sprinkle with ¼ cup grated Parmesan, then place in a preheated oven, 400°F, for about 15 minutes or until golden and bubbling.

Goat Cheese and Sundried Tomato Ravioli with Basil Oil

Serves 2

1 freshly rolled large pasta sheet, or 24 gyoza or wonton wrappers
flour, for dusting
1 egg yolk, for brushing

For the filling

5 oz soft goat cheese
6 tablespoons mascarpone cheese
3 sundried tomatoes in oil, drained and finely chopped
salt and pepper

For the basil oil

⅔ cup basil leaves
5 tablespoons extra virgin olive oil

- To make the filling, mix together the cheeses and sundried tomatoes in a bowl and season well with salt and pepper.

- To make the basil oil, place the basil and oil in a small food processor or blender and whiz together, then pass through a very fine sieve to form a green oil.

- Lay the pasta sheet on a clean work surface lightly dusted with flour. Using a plain 2 in cutter, stamp out 24 rounds from the sheets. Place a heaping tablespoon of filling in the center of a pasta round or wrapper and then brush a little egg around the edges. Brush the edge of a second round or wrapper and place it, moist edge down, over the filling. Gently press out any excess air and use your fingers to seal. Place on a baking sheet lightly dusted with flour. Repeat with the remaining rounds or wrappers and filling.

- Cook the pasta in a large saucepan of salted boiling water for 3 minutes or until cooked through. Remove from the pan with a slotted spoon and arrange on a serving plate. Drizzle with the oil and serve immediately.

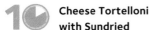

1 Cheese Tortelloni with Sundried Tomato Pesto Place a handful of basil leaves, 3 tablespoons toasted pine nuts, 5 drained sundried tomatoes in oil, 2 tablespoons grated Parmesan cheese, and 3 tablespoons olive oil in a small food processor or blender and whiz to form a pesto. Cook 8 oz cheese tortelloni according to the package instructions. Drain and return to the pan. Stir through the sundried tomato pesto and serve immediately.

2 Goat Cheese and Tomato Penne Heat a little olive oil in a skillet, add 1 chopped onion, and cook over low heat until softened. Stir in 1 chopped garlic clove, then pour over a 13 oz can tomatoes and simmer for 15 minutes. Meanwhile, cook 14 oz penne according to the package instructions until al dente. Mash 4 oz soft goat cheese in a bowl. Pour over a little of the tomato sauce and stir until the cheese melts. Add 4 cups chopped baby spinach leaves and ½ cup pitted black olives to the tomato sauce, followed by the warmed cheese. Drain the pasta and return to the pan, then toss through the sauce. Serve with extra cheese crumbled over, if desired.

30 Lamb Chops with Garlicky Zucchini and Anchovy Tagliatelle

Serves 4

2 tablespoons butter

3 tablespoons olive oil, plus extra for brushing

4 garlic cloves, crushed

8 anchovy fillets in oil, drained

1 rosemary sprig, leaves stripped and finely chopped

1 zucchini, thinly sliced

8 lamb chops

14 oz tagliatelle

handful of flat-leaf parsley, chopped

salt and pepper

- Melt the butter in a small saucepan, then add the oil and garlic and cook over low heat for 5 minutes until softened, taking care not to burn the garlic. Add the anchovies and rosemary and cook for a couple more minutes, mashing with the back of a spoon until the anchovies melt.

- Heat a griddle pan until smoking hot. Brush the zucchini slices with a little oil and cook for 3 minutes on each side until golden. Remove to a plate and keep warm. Brush the lamb chops with a little oil and season well with salt and pepper. Cook for 5–7 minutes, turn over, and cook for an additional 5 minutes or until charred and cooked through.

- Cook the pasta in a large pan of salted boiling water according to the package instructions until al dente. Drain, reserving some cooking water, and return to the pan. Add the garlic and anchovy oil and toss through, stirring in a little cooking water to loosen if needed, then stir in the zucchini and parsley. Pile onto serving plates, arrange the lamb chops alongside, and serve immediately.

 Quick Zucchini and Anchovy Tagliatelle
Cook and drain the tagliatelle as above. Meanwhile, heat a little olive oil in a skillet, add 2 chopped garlic cloves and cook for 30 seconds, then add 6 drained anchovy fillets in oil and cook for an additional 2 minutes, mashing with the back of a spoon. Pour over 3 tablespoons heavy cream and heat through. Finely grate 2 zucchini and stir through the drained pasta with the sauce. Serve immediately.

 Lamb and Red Pepper Tagliatelle with Anchovy Sauce Cut 10 oz lamb chops into thin strips. Heat a little olive oil in a skillet, add the lamb, and cook over high heat until golden all over and just cooked through. Remove from the pan and set aside. Add the garlic and anchovies to the pan and cook as above. Meanwhile, cook and drain the tagliatelle as above. Slice 1 drained roasted red pepper from a jar into thin strips and stir through the drained pasta with the fried lamb and anchovy oil. Serve immediately.

PAS-FOOD-WON

Spaghetti with Angler Fish, Mussels, and Fennel

Serves 4

3 tablespoons boiling water
½ teaspoon saffron threads
1 tablespoon butter
1 fennel bulb, sliced
3 tablespoons dry white wine
1 lb mussels, debearded and
   cleaned
⅔ cup sour cream
1 tablespoon olive oil
10 oz angler Fish fillet, boned and
   cut into ¾ inch thick slices
14 oz spaghetti
salt and pepper
chopped tarragon leaves,
   to garnish

· Pour the measurement water over the saffron in a heatproof bowl and allow to infuse.

· Heat the butter in a large saucepan, add the fennel, and cook over medium heat for 5 minutes until softened. Pour over the wine and saffron with the soaking liquid and add the mussels. Cover with a lid and cook for 5 minutes until the mussels have opened. Discard any that remain closed. Stir through the sour cream and season well with salt and pepper.

· Meanwhile, heat the oil in a nonstick skillet, add the anglerfish and cook over high heat for 3 minutes on each side or until just cooked through. Carefully stir the angler fish into the mussel sauce.

· While the mussel sauce is cooking, cook the pasta in a large saucepan of salted boiling water according to the package instructions until al dente. Drain, reserving a little of the cooking water. Stir through the mussel sauce, adding a little cooking water if needed, and season.

· Spoon into serving bowls and serve sprinkled with the tarragon.

Quick Angler Fish Spaghetti Cook the angler fish, as above, under a preheated hot broiler for 3–5 minutes on each side. Meanwhile, cook and drain the spaghetti as above. Stir through the angler fish, 1 chopped tomato, ½ chopped red chili, seeded if desired, a squeeze of lemon juice, and a handful of chopped flat-leaf parsley. Serve immediately.

Spaghetti with Pancetta-wrapped Anglerfish Cut a 13 oz piece of angler fish in half lengthwise, removing any bone. Lay the two halves on top of each other to make a slab of even thickness, then wrap 8 pancetta slices around to secure the two halves. Cook under a preheated hot broiler for 7–10 minutes, then turn over and cook for an additional 7–10 minutes or until the fish is just cooked through. Meanwhile, prepare the saffron threads as above and allow to infuse for 10 minutes, then mix together with 3 tablespoons heavy cream. While the saffron is infusing, cook and drain the spaghetti as above. Cut the angler fish into slices, adding any juices to the saffron sauce. Toss the sauce through the drained pasta and serve alongside the fish.

3 Summery Sausage Pasta

Serves 4

4 tablespoons olive oil
6 large pork sausages
2 onions, sliced
2 red and 2 yellow bell peppers,
  cored, seeded, and sliced
1 garlic clove, crushed
1 tablespoon tomato paste
2 teaspoons sugar
1 tablespoon balsamic vinegar
3 large tomatoes, chopped
2 tablespoons water
handful of basil leaves, chopped,
  plus extra to garnish
14 oz radiatore pasta
salt and pepper

- Grease a baking sheet with 1 tablespoon of the oil, add the sausages, and place in a preheated oven, 400°F, for 20–25 minutes, until brown and cooked through.

- Meanwhile, heat the remaining oil in a saucepan, add the onions and cook for 5 minutes until softened. Add the peppers, garlic, tomato paste, sugar, vinegar, tomatoes, paste, and measurement water. Cover and cook for 15 minutes. Remove the lid and cook for an additional 5 minutes until the peppers are really soft. Season well with salt and pepper and stir through the basil.

- While the sausages and peppers are cooking, cook the pasta in a large saucepan of salted boiling water according to the package instructions until al dente. Drain, reserving a little of the cooking water, and return to the pan.

- Slice the sausages into bite-size pieces. Stir through the pasta with the peppers, adding a little cooking water to loosen if needed. Season well. Spoon into serving bowls and serve sprinkled with extra chopped basil.

---

1 **Winter Sausage Pasta** Steam ½ head of thinly sliced cabbage over a saucepan of boiling water for 10 minutes until soft. Meanwhile, cook 14 oz fusilli according to the package instructions until al dente. Drain the pasta and return to the pan. Stir through the cabbage, 3 smoked sausages (such as kielbasa), sliced, a knob of butter, and ¼ cup grated Parmesan cheese. Serve immediately.

2 **Spanish-Style Sausage Pasta** Rub 2 tablespoons olive oil over 4 red bell peppers and cook under a preheated hot broiler for 10 minutes, turning frequently, until charred all over. Place in a plastic food bag, seal, and leave for 5 minutes. When cooled, peel away the blackened skin. Cut in half, remove the seeds, and slice. Meanwhile, cook the radiatore as above. Heat 1 tablespoon olive oil in a skillet, add 5 oz chorizo sausage, cut into chunks, and sizzle for a couple of minutes. Add the sliced peppers and a splash of water, season well, and cook for a few minutes more. Drain the pasta and return to the pan. Toss through the chorizo and peppers and serve with shavings of Manchego cheese.

 # Seared Sea Bass with Warm Pasta Salad and Basil Oil

Serves 4

2 tablespoons olive oil
4 small sea bass fillets, boned
10 oz fregola pasta
squeeze of lemon juice
⅓ cup sun-blush tomatoes
  in oil, drained and chopped
⅓ cup pitted black olives
salt and pepper

For the basil oil

6 tablespoons extra virgin
  olive oil
large handful of basil leaves,
  roughly chopped
1 garlic clove

- To make the basil oil, place the extra virgin olive oil in a small saucepan, add the basil and garlic, and cook over low heat for 10 minutes. Allow to cool, then pass the flavored oil through a sieve.

- Heat the oil in a large nonstick skillet, add the sea bass, skin side down, and cook over high heat for 5–7 minutes until golden and crisp. Carefully turn over, season well with salt and pepper, and cook for an additional 3–5 minutes or until the fish is opaque and cooked through. Slice each fillet in half.

- Meanwhile, cook the pasta in a large saucepan of salted boiling water according to the package instructions until al dente. Drain well. Stir in 2 tablespoons of the basil oil, a good squeeze of lemon juice, the tomatoes, and olives and season.

- Arrange the fish alongside the pasta salad on serving plates and drizzle over the remaining basil oil.

---

 1 **Olive and Pesto Pasta with Pan-Fried Sea Bass** Cook the fregola pasta as above. Meanwhile, cut 4 boned sea bass fillets into thin strips and fry in a little olive oil in a skillet for 3 minutes on each side or until just cooked through. Drain the pasta and return to the pan. Stir through 4 tablespoons store-bought fresh green pesto and a handful of pitted black olives. Pile the pasta into serving bowls, arrange the fish strips on top and then sprinkle with 1 chopped tomato. Serve immediately.

3 **Olive and Tomato Pasta with Poached Sea Bass** Put 1 tablespoon red wine vinegar and 1 crushed garlic clove in a bowl, then stir in 5 chopped tomatoes and allow to stand for at least 20 minutes. Meanwhile, chop 1 onion, 1 celery stick, and 1 carrot, and add to a shallow skillet with a couple of peppercorns, 1 bay leaf, 1 sliced lemon, and about 4 cups water. Bring to a boil, then reduce the heat and simmer for 10 minutes. Add 4 boned sea bass fillets, and poach for 10 minutes or until cooked and the fish flakes easily. While the fish is poaching, cook and drain the fregola pasta as above. Remove the skin from the sea bass, break into flakes, and add to the pasta with the chopped tomatoes, a handful of chopped basil leaves, and a handful of pitted black olives. Serve immediately.

Fiery Black Spaghetti with Squid

Serves 4

14 oz black squid ink spaghetti
4 tablespoons olive oil, plus extra
   to serve
14 oz prepared squid, cleaned and
   sliced into rings
4 garlic cloves, sliced
1 red chili, seeded, if desired,
   and sliced
juice of 1 lemon
handful of basil leaves, chopped
salt and pepper

- Cook the pasta in a large saucepan of salted boiling water according to the package instructions until al dente.

- Meanwhile, heat the oil in a large skillet. Pat the squid rings dry with paper towels, then add to the pan and cook over high heat for about 30 seconds until starting to brown. Add the garlic and chili and cook for a couple of seconds, taking care not to let the garlic burn. The squid should be white and just cooked through. Squeeze over the lemon juice and season with salt and pepper to taste.

- Drain the pasta and return to the pan. Toss through the squid and basil, and olive oil to taste. Serve immediately.

---

2 **Lemony Black Spaghetti with Seared Squid** Heat a little butter in a saucepan, add 1 finely chopped shallot and 3 sliced garlic cloves, and cook gently until soft. Squeeze over the juice of 1 lemon, then, over low heat, whisk in 3½ tablespoons cold butter, cubed. Sprinkle with torn basil leaves and set aside. Cook the squid ink spaghetti as above. Cut 8 prepared and cleaned small squid in half. Score each half to make a criss-cross pattern. Toss in a little olive oil and salt. Cook on a preheated hot griddle pan for 2 minutes, turning until charring and curling up. Drain the pasta, toss through the lemon sauce. Serve with the squid and sprinkle with dried red pepper flakes and extra chopped basil.

3 **Fiery Black Spaghetti and Seafood Packets** Parboil the squid ink spaghetti for 5 minutes in a large saucepan of salted boiling water, then drain, cool under cold water, and drain again. Meanwhile, fry the chili and garlic in the oil in a large saucepan as above, pour over 3 tablespoons dry white wine and cook for a couple of minutes. Add 4 chopped tomatoes, 5 oz cleaned clams, and 5 oz debearded and cleaned mussels, cover with a lid, and cook for an additional 5 minutes until the shells have opened. Discard any that remain closed. Add the squid, prepared as above, and spaghetti and season to taste. Divide the mixture between 4 large squares of foil, then lift up the edges and fold over to seal. Place on a baking sheet and cook in a preheated oven, 400°F, for 10 minutes or until the pasta and squid are cooked through. Tear open with a knife and serve sprinkled with some chopped basil leaves.

30 Venison and Chestnut Gnocchetti Sardi

Serves 4

1 tablespoon olive oil

6 large venison sausages

1 garlic clove, finely chopped

1 rosemary sprig

1 teaspoon tomato paste

5 tablespoons red wine

6 tablespoons hot chicken or
   game stock

¾ cup store-bought cooked and
   peeled chestnuts, halved

14 oz gnocchetti
   sardi pasta

5 tablespoons heavy cream

salt and pepper

chopped flat-leaf parsley,
   to garnish

- Heat the oil in a pan, add the sausages, and cook over medium heat until golden all over. Remove from the pan, cool slightly, and cut into bite-size pieces. Add the garlic, rosemary, and tomato purée to the pan and cook for a couple of minutes, stirring continuously.

- Pour over the wine and bubble until reduced by half. Add the stock, return the sausages to the pan, add the chestnuts, and simmer for 20 minutes until the sausages are cooked.

- Meanwhile, cook the pasta in a large saucepan of salted boiling water according to the package instructions until al dente. Drain, reserving a little of the cooking water, and return to the pan. Add the cream to the sausage sauce and season with salt and pepper. Heat through, then stir into the pasta, adding a little cooking water if needed. Spoon into serving bowls and serve sprinkled with the parsley.

---

1 **Fusilli with Chestnut Sauce and Bacon** Cook 14 oz fusilli according to the package instructions until al dente. Meanwhile, cook 4 bacon slices under a preheated medium broiler for 7 minutes or until crisp. Cut into bite-size pieces. Heat a little olive oil in a skillet, add 1 chopped garlic clove, and cook for 30 seconds. Roughly chop the chestnuts, add the chestnuts, 3 tablespoons hot chicken stock, and 3 tablespoons heavy cream and simmer for 5 minutes. Drain the pasta and return to the pan, then stir through the chestnut sauce, bacon, and a handful of chopped flat-leaf parsley. Serve immediately.

2 **Chicken Liver Pasta** Cut 7 oz chicken livers into small pieces, discarding any membrane. Heat a little olive oil in a skillet, add 2 finely chopped garlic cloves, and cook for 30 seconds, then add the chicken livers and cook for an additional 3 minutes until golden and just cooked through. Add 5 tablespoons dry white wine and cook for a couple of minutes until reduced down. Meanwhile, cook and drain the gnocchetti sardi pasta as above. Stir through the chicken livers and a handful of grated Parmesan cheese. Serve immediately.

3 Blue Cheese and Cauliflower Cannelloni

Serves 8

1 head of cauliflower, cut into florets
⅓ cup walnuts
12 fresh lasagna sheets
¾ cup cream cheese
5 oz blue cheese, such as Gorgonzola
oil, for greasing
1 cup sour cream
5 tablespoons milk
¼ cup grated Parmesan cheese
salt and pepper
watercress salad, to serve

- Cook the cauliflower in a saucepan of boiling water for 7–10 minutes until cooked through. Drain loosely and return to the pan. Mash to a rough paste and allow to cool slightly.

- Place the walnuts in a small skillet and dry-fry for 3 minutes or until lightly golden, then roughly chop. Prepare the lasagna sheets, if necessary, according to the package instructions.

- Mix together the cooled cauliflower, cream cheese, and blue cheese in a bowl. Spoon a little filling along the length of each sheet, then roll up and place in a large greased ovenproof dish.

- Mix together the sour cream and milk in a bowl until smooth, season with salt and pepper, and pour over the cannelloni. Sprinkle with the Parmesan and walnuts.

- Place in a preheated oven, 400°F, for 10–15 minutes or until golden, bubbling, and heated through. Serve with a watercress salad.

---

1 Cauliflower Penne with Blue Cheese

Prepare and cook 1 head of cauliflower, as above, and add 1 lb fresh penne to the water to cook until al dente. The cauliflower should be just tender and the pasta al dente. Add 4½ cups baby spinach leaves to the pan just before draining. Drain and return to the pan, then toss together with 5 oz chopped blue cheese and a dollop of sour cream. Serve.

2 Cauliflower Pasta and Blue Cheese Soup with Watercress Pesto

Heat a little olive oil in a large saucepan, add the cauliflower, prepared as above, and 1 small chopped onion, and cook over low heat for 5–10 minutes until softened. Pour over 2½ cups hot vegetable stock and bring to a boil. Reduce the heat and simmer for 10 minutes. Remove from the heat, then blend together with an immersion blender. Return to the heat and add a good dollop of sour cream and 4 oz chopped blue cheese. Meanwhile, cook 4 oz ditalini according to the package instructions. Drain, then add to the soup for 1 minute. Place 2½ cups watercress, 2 tablespoons walnuts, ¼ cup grated Parmesan cheese, and 3 tablespoons extra virgin olive oil in a food processor or blender and whiz together to form a pesto. Ladle the soup into bowls and spoon over the pesto to serve.

Mafaldine with Rich Confit Duck and Pancetta

Serves 4

3 tablespoons olive oil
1 onion, finely chopped
1 carrot, peeled and finely chopped
1 celery stick, finely chopped
1 garlic clove, crushed
1 tablespoon tomato paste
5 tablespoons dry white wine
13 oz can chopped tomatoes
2 strips of orange peel
¾ cup water
1 bay leaf
1 thyme sprig
4 oz pancetta cubes
4 confit duck legs
14 oz mafaldine
salt and pepper

· Heat 2 tablespoons of the oil in a large saucepan, add the onion, carrot, and celery, and cook gently for 5 minutes until softened. Stir in the garlic and tomato paste and cook for 1 minute more.

· Pour over the wine, increase the heat, and bubble vigorously for a couple of minutes until reduced, then stir in the tomatoes, orange peel, and measurement water. Add the herbs, bring to a boil, and cook for 15 minutes.

· Remove the pan from the heat. Remove the orange peel and herbs then, using an immersion blender, whiz to form a smooth sauce. Return to the heat.

· Meanwhile, heat the remaining oil in a skillet, add the pancetta and cook until golden. Using a fork, tear the duck into shreds, then add to the sauce with the pancetta and simmer for 5 minutes.

· While the sauce is cooking, cook the pasta in a large saucepan of salted boiling water according to the package instructions until al dente. Drain, reserving a little of the cooking water, and return to the pan. Stir through the sauce, adding a little cooking water to loosen if needed. Season with salt and pepper to taste and serve immediately.

---

1 **Quick Confit Duck and Red Pepper Mafaldine** Cook and drain the mafaldine as above. Meanwhile, cut 4 confit duck legs and 2 drained roasted red peppers from a jar into bite-size pieces. Toss the duck and peppers through the drained pasta with 5 tablespoons sour cream and 2½ cups watercress. Serve immediately.

2 **Easy Confit Duck Mafaldine** Pick the meat off 4 confit duck legs. Heat a little olive oil in a skillet, add the duck and 2 finely chopped garlic cloves, and cook over medium heat for 5 minutes until sizzling. Pour over 3 tablespoons dry white wine and 5 tablespoons hot chicken stock and cook for 10 minutes until reduced down, then stir in 3 tablespoons sour cream fraîche. Meanwhile, cook and drain the mafaldine as above, then stir through the sauce and a large handful of chopped arugula leaves. Serve immediately.

Creamy Asparagus Pasta

Serves 4

14 oz cappellacci
1 bunch of asparagus, trimmed
1 tablespoon butter
1 garlic clove, sliced
5 oz mixed wild mushrooms,
    trimmed and halved if large
5 tablespoons sour cream
salt and pepper
Parmesan cheese shavings,
    to serve

· Cook the pasta in a large saucepan of salted boiling water according to the package instructions until al dente. Add the asparagus 3 minutes before the end of the cooking time and cook until just tender.

· Meanwhile, heat the butter in a skillet, add the garlic and cook for 1 minute, then stir in the mushrooms and cook for 5 minutes until soft and golden. Stir in the sour cream.

· Drain the pasta and asparagus, reserving a little of the cooking water, and return to the pan. Stir through the mushroom sauce and season with salt and pepper, adding a little cooking water to loosen if needed. Spoon into serving bowls and serve sprinkled with the Parmesan shavings.

10 Asparagus Linguine with Lemon Carbonara Sauce

Cook 14 oz linguine according to the package instructions until al dente, adding the asparagus as above. Meanwhile, mix together 1 egg, 3 tablespoons sour cream and a good squeeze of lemon juice in a bowl. Drain the pasta and asparagus and return to the pan. Toss through the egg sauce and serve immediately.

30 Asparagus and Bacon Pasta Bake

Cook 12 oz penne according to the package instructions until al dente, adding the asparagus as above. Meanwhile, cook 5 bacon slices under a preheated medium broiler for 10 minutes until cooked through. Cool for 1 minute, then cut into small pieces. Drain the pasta and asparagus and return to the pan. Mix together 5 oz soft goat cheese with enough milk to make a smooth sauce, then stir through the drained pasta with the bacon. Spoon into an ovenproof dish and top with a handful of grated Gruyère cheese. Place in a preheated oven, 400°F, for 15 minutes or until golden and bubbling.

30 Linguine with Creamy Marsala Chicken

Serves 4

3 tablespoons olive oil
2 boneless chicken breasts
1 shallot, finely sliced
⅔ cup Marsala
⅔ cup hot chicken stock
1 sage leaf, finely chopped
6 tablespoons heavy cream
7 oz chestnut mushrooms,
    trimmed and halved if large
14 oz linguine
salt and pepper
chopped flat-leaf parsley,
    to garnish

- Heat 1 tablespoon of the oil in a skillet. Season the chicken breasts with salt and pepper, add to the pan and cook for 5–7 minutes on each side or until golden and cooked through.

- Meanwhile, heat 1 tablespoon of the oil in a saucepan, add the shallot, and cook over low heat for a couple of minutes until softened. Pour over the Marsala, increase the heat to high, and cook for a couple of minutes until reduced and slightly syrupy. Add the stock and sage and simmer for an additional 5 minutes. Stir in the cream, season well, and keep warm.

- Cut the chicken into slices and add to the sauce. Add the remaining oil to the skillet and cook the mushrooms for 3–5 minutes until golden all over, then stir into the sauce.

- Meanwhile, cook the pasta in a large pan of salted boiling water according to the package instructions. Drain, reserving a little of the cooking water, and return to the pan. Toss through the sauce, adding cooking water to loosen if needed. Season and serve sprinkled with parsley.

 Quick Marsala Chicken Linguine

Cook the linguine as above. Meanwhile, heat a little butter in a skillet, add 1 chopped garlic clove, and cook for 30 seconds. Add the mushrooms as above and cook until golden, then add 2 store-bought roasted chicken breasts, skin discarded and torn into shreds, and a splash of Marsala and cook for a couple of minutes. Drain the pasta and return to the pan. Toss through the chicken mixture with 4 tablespoons heavy cream. Serve immediately.

 Linguine with Poached Chicken

in Marsala Place 2 boneless, skinless chicken breasts in a pan and pour over 6 tablespoons Marsala and enough chicken stock to cover, then poach gently for 15 minutes or until just cooked through. Meanwhile, cook and drain the linguine and fry the mushrooms as above. Cut the chicken into strips and stir through the drained pasta with the mushrooms, a little of the poaching liquid (boiled down if liked) to loosen, and some heavy cream. Serve at once.

Macaroni Shrimp Gratin

Serves 6

3 egg yolks
juice of 1 lemon
14 tablespoons butter, melted
6 tablespoons heavy cream
1¼ lb elbow macaroni
3 tablespoons olive oil
3 leeks, trimmed, cleaned,
  and sliced
10 oz large cooked peeled shrimp
salt and pepper

- Place the egg yolks in a heatproof bowl that will snugly fit over a saucepan of simmering water (make sure the bottom of the bowl doesn't touch the water). Add most of the lemon juice then, very slowly, start to pour in the butter, whisking continuously. As the butter thickens the sauce, you can add it a little quicker. When the sauce has thickened and is the consistency of mayonnaise, remove from the pan. Allow to cool, season well with salt and pepper, and add more lemon juice to taste. Whip the cream until soft peaks form, then carefully fold into the sauce.

- Meanwhile, cook the pasta in a large saucepan of salted boiling water according to the pack instructions until al dente.

- Heat the oil in a saucepan, add the leeks with a splash of water, and cook gently for about 7 minutes until beginning to soften. Add the shrimp and cook for 2 minutes or until heated through.

- Drain the pasta and return to the pan, then mix through the sauce, leeks, and shrimp and season. Spoon into individual gratin dishes and cook under a preheated hot broiler for 3–5 minutes or until lightly browned all over.

 Quick Shrimp and Leek Pasta Cook the leeks and shrimp as above. Meanwhile, cook 1¼ lb chifferi according to the package instructions until al dente. Drain and return to the pan. Stir through the shrimp mixture, 5 tablespoons sour cream, and a good squeeze of lemon juice. Serve sprinkled with chopped basil.

Tropical Shrimp Fusilli Heat a little olive oil in a large skillet, add 1 chopped garlic clove and ½ seeded and chopped red chili, and cook for 30 seconds until golden. Add 3 leeks, trimmed, cleaned, and sliced, and cook for 5 minutes more. Pour over a 13 oz can chopped tomatoes and 6 tablespoons hot vegetable or fish stock, then cook for 10 minutes until softened and reduced. Add the grated zest and juice of 1 lime and 6 tablespoons heavy cream. Simmer for an additional 1–2 minutes, then add 10 oz large cooked peeled shrimp and heat through. Meanwhile, cook 1¼ lb fusilli according to the package instructions until al dente. Drain and return to the pan, then toss through the sauce with a handful of chopped basil leaves.

2 Pasta with Salmon, Arugula, and Red Onion

Serves 4

14 oz casareccia pasta
6 tablespoons dry white wine
⅔ cup heavy cream
8 oz smoked salmon,
  cut into strips
2 cups arugula leaves
½ red onion, thinly sliced
grated zest of ½ lemon
2 teaspoons capers, rinsed
  and drained
salt and pepper

- Cook the pasta in a large saucepan of salted boiling water according to the package instructions until al dente.

- Meanwhile, heat the wine in a saucepan until boiling, then reduce the heat and simmer for 5 minutes. Stir through the cream, season with salt and pepper, and allow to bubble for a couple of minutes.

- Drain the pasta, reserving a little of the cooking water, and return to the pan. Stir through the sauce, adding a little cooking water to loosen if needed. Toss through the remaining ingredients and serve immediately.

 Salmon, Red Onion, and Arugula Pasta Salad Cook 10 oz orzo according to the package instructions. Drain, then cool under cold running water and drain again. Meanwhile, mix together 2 tablespoons plain yogurt, 4 tablespoons mayonnaise, and plenty of black pepper in a bowl. Tip the pasta into a serving dish and stir through the yogurt with the smoked salmon, arugula, onion, lemon zest, and capers as above.

 Pasta with Honey-Roasted Salmon Drizzle 1 tablespoon honey and a good grinding of black pepper over 2 thick salmon fillets. Place in a preheated oven, 400°F, for 12–15 minutes or until the fish is cooked through and flakes easily. Meanwhile, cook the casareccia pasta as above. Heat a little olive oil in a skillet, add 1 chopped red onion, and cook until softened, then pour over 5 tablespoons dry white wine and simmer until reduced.

Add 1 teaspoon Dijon mustard, the grated zest of ½ lemon, and 5 tablespoons heavy cream and heat through. Drain the pasta and return to the pan. Remove any skin and bones from the salmon, then flake and add to the sauce. Toss the sauce through the drained pasta with 2 cups arugula leaves and serve immediately.

3⬤ Creamy Lobster Fettuccine

Serves 2

2 tablespoons butter
2 shallots, finely chopped
1 teaspoon tomato paste
1 large cooked lobster
2 tablespoons brandy
⅔ cup Madeira
5 tablespoons heavy cream
1 egg yolk
pinch of cayenne pepper
7 oz fettuccine
salt and pepper
chopped tarragon leaves,
   to garnish

- Heat the butter in a large skillet, add the shallots, and cook over low heat until softened. Stir in the tomato paste and cook for 1 minute. Meanwhile, remove the lobster meat from the shell and cut the tails in half. Add the lobster shell to the skillet and cook for 5–10 minutes until browned.

- Remove the pan from the heat and add the brandy. Return to the heat and boil vigorously until reduced down. Pour over the Madeira and bubble for 5–10 minutes until reduced by half. Pass through a sieve, pressing down hard to extract the juices.

- Return the sauce to the pan. Mix together the cream, egg yolk, and cayenne pepper. Add a tablespoon of the sauce to the cream mixture to warm a little, then stir the cream into the pan. Heat through but do not let it boil, then add the lobster meat.

- Meanwhile, cook the pasta in a large saucepan of salted boiling water according to the package instructions until al dente. Drain, reserving a little of the cooking water, and return to the pan. Toss the sauce through the pasta until coated all over, adding a little cooking water to loosen if needed, and season with salt and pepper.

- Spoon into serving bowls, top with the lobster tail and serve sprinkled with the tarragon.

 Quick Lobster Fettuccine Cook the fettuccine as above. Drain, reserving a little of the cooking water, and return to the pan. Stir through 7 oz potted lobster, 1 egg yolk, and a handful of chopped tarragon leaves and serve immediately.

 Lobster Pasta Salad Cook 7 oz orzo according to the package instructions. Drain, then cool under cold running water and drain again. Stir together 3 tablespoons mayonnaise, 3 tablespoons sour cream, the grated zest and juice of ½ lemon, 1 finely chopped shallot, and a handful of chopped chives and tarragon in a bowl. Stir in the chopped lobster meat from 1 cooked lobster. Tip the pasta into a serving dish and toss together with the lobster mixture and a large handful of arugula leaves.

30 Pappardelle with Chestnuts, Arugula and Prosciutto

Serves 4

5 tablespoons olive oil, plus extra to serve
6 sage leaves
rind of ½ lemon, cut into strips
¾ cup store-bought cooked and peeled chestnuts, halved if desired
14 oz pappardelle
juice of ½ lemon
1¼ cups arugula leaves
5 oz prosciutto
salt

- Place the oil in a medium pan, add the sage leaves and lemon rind, and heat very gently for about 10 minutes. Add the chestnuts and cook gently for an additional 10 minutes. Remove from the heat and set aside for 10 minutes.

- Meanwhile, cook the pasta in a large saucepan of salted boiling water according to the package instructions until al dente. Drain.

- Remove the lemon rind and sage leaves from the oil. Toss together the chestnut lemon oil with the pasta.

- Pile onto serving plates and arrange the arugula and prosciutto on top. Serve immediately with a squeeze of lemon juice over each portion.

 1 Simple Prosciutto and Chestnut Pappardelle Cook and drain the pappardelle as above. Meanwhile, heat a little olive oil in a skillet, add the prosciutto, and cook until sizzling. Remove from the pan and add the chestnuts, prepared as above, and 1 sliced garlic clove. Cook for an additional 3 minutes until golden. Squeeze over the juice and grated zest of 1 lemon, then toss through the drained pasta with the prosciutto, broken into small pieces. Serve sprinkled with chopped flat-leaf parsley.

 2 Creamy Chestnut and Mushroom Pappardelle Soak ⅔ cup porcini mushrooms in a little boiling water for 15 minutes or until soft. Meanwhile, heat a little butter in a skillet, add 1 chopped shallot, and cook gently until softened. Pour over 3 tablespoons Marsala and bubble until reduced. Add ⅔ cup hot chicken stock and the chestnuts, prepared as above, and simmer for 10 minutes until softened. While the sauce is cooking, cook and drain the pappardelle as above. Stir the mushrooms and soaking liquid into the sauce, cook for an additional couple of minutes, then add 3 tablespoons heavy cream and toss through the drained pasta and top with prosciutto.

3⃝ Creamy Tomato Pasta with Shrimp

Serves 4

2 tablespoons butter
1 onion, finely chopped
1 celery stick, finely chopped
1 garlic clove, finely chopped
1 teaspoon fennel seeds
⅔ cup dry white wine
1 tablespoon brandy
13 oz can chopped tomatoes
1 thyme sprig
1 bay leaf
3 tablespoons heavy cream
14 oz cannelli pasta
1 tablespoon olive oil
8 large raw unpeeled shrimp
salt and pepper
chopped basil leaves, to garnish

- Heat the butter in a saucepan, add the onion, celery, and garlic, and cook over low heat for 5 minutes or until softened. Add the fennel and cook for 30 seconds more.

- Remove from the heat, then pour over the wine and brandy. Return to the heat and cook over high heat for a couple of minutes until reduced down, then add the tomatoes and herbs and simmer for 15–20 minutes, adding a little water if needed.

- Remove the pan from the heat. Discard the herbs, then using an immersion blender, whiz to form a smooth sauce. Stir through the cream and season with salt and pepper. Meanwhile, cook the pasta in a large saucepan of salted boiling water according to the pack instructions until al dente.

- Heat the oil in a large skillet, add the shrimp and cook for 3 minutes on each side or until pink and cooked through. Drain the pasta, reserving a little of the cooking water. Toss through the sauce, adding a little cooking water to loosen if needed. Spoon into bowls and top with the shrimp. Serve sprinkled with the basil.

 Simple Shrimp and Tomato Spaghetti

Cook 14 oz spaghetti according to the pack instructions until al dente. Meanwhile, cook the shrimp as above under a preheated hot broiler for about 3–5 minutes or until they turn pink and are cooked through. Drain the pasta and return to the pan. Stir through the shrimp, 3½ tablespoons garlic butter, 2 chopped tomatoes, and the grated zest of 1 lemon. Serve immediately.

 Shrimp and Tomato Pasta

Heat a little olive oil in a large skillet, add 1 teaspoon fennel seeds and 2 sliced garlic cloves, and cook for 30 seconds. Add 14 oz halved baby plum tomatoes, a splash of dry white wine, and a little water and simmer for 10 minutes. Stir through the shrimp as above and cook for 3–5 minutes or until they turn pink and are cooked through, then stir in 3 tablespoons mascarpone cheese. Meanwhile, cook and drain the canelli pasta as above. Stir through the shrimp sauce with a handful of chopped basil leaves. Serve immediately.

Tagliarelle with Seared Steak and Goulash Sauce

Serves 4

2 tablespoons olive oil
1 onion, thinly sliced
1 red bell pepper, cored, seeded, and chopped
1 tablespoon smoked paprika
13 oz can chopped tomatoes
2 thick beef steaks
11 oz tagliarelle
3 tablespoons sour cream
salt and pepper

- Heat 1 tablespoon of the oil in a large saucepan, add the onion, and cook gently for a couple of minutes until softened. Stir in the red pepper and cook for an additional 5 minutes until softened. Add the paprika and tomatoes, then season well with salt and pepper. Bring to a boil, reduce the heat, and simmer for 15 minutes.

- Meanwhile, heat a griddle pan until smoking hot. Rub the remaining oil over the beef steaks and season well. Add to the pan and cook for 2–4 minutes on each side so it it hot through. Allow to rest for 5 minutes and cut into bite-size pieces. Cook the pasta in a large saucepan of salted boiling water according to the package instructions until al dente. Drain, reserving a little cooking water, and return to the pan.

- Stir the chopped steak and half of the sour cream into the tomato sauce, mix into the pasta, adding a little cooking water to loosen if needed. Pile the pasta onto serving plates and dollop over the remaining cream. Serve.

 Quick Stir-Fried Beef and Red Pepper Tagliarelle Heat a little olive oil in a wok or large skillet, add 1 chopped garlic clove and 10 oz stir-fry beef strips, and stir-fry for a minute or two, then add a pinch of dried red pepper flakes, ½ cup cherry tomatoes, halved, and 1 drained, chopped roasted red pepper from a jar. Add a splash of water and cook over high heat until cooked through. Meanwhile, cook and drain the tagliarelle as above. Toss through the beef mixture. Top with plain yogurt.

Tagliarelle with Seared Steak and Pizzaiola Sauce Heat a little olive oil in a skillet, add 10 oz sirloin steak, and cook over high heat for 5 minutes until browned all over. Remove from the pan and allow to rest. Add a 13 oz can chopped tomatoes, 1 crushed garlic clove, 1 teaspoon dried oregano and a handful of pitted black olives to the pan and bubble for about 10 minutes until thickened. Meanwhile, cook and drain the tagliarelle as above. Cut the steak into slices, stir through the sauce and then add to the drained pasta. Serve immediately.

Sweet Potato Pockets with Sage Butter and Amaretti

Serves 4

1 freshly rolled large fresh
    pasta sheet, or 24 gyoza or
    wonton wrappers
flour, for dusting
1 egg yolk, for brushing
2 amaretti cookies, crumbled

For the filling

3 small sweet potatoes, peeled
    and chopped
6 tablespoons Parmesan
    cheese, grated
grating of nutmeg
salt and pepper

For the sage butter

3½ tablespoons butter
8 sage leaves

- To make the filling, cook the sweet potato in a large saucepan of boiling water for 10 minutes or until just soft, then drain well. Allow to cool slightly, then mix together with the cheese and nutmeg in a bowl and season with salt and pepper to taste.

- Lay the pasta sheet on a clean work surface lightly dusted with flour, then cut out 12 x 1 inch squares and 12 x 1½ inch squares. Alternatively, use gyoza or wonton wrappers. Place a heaping tablespoon of filling in the center of a smaller square or wrapper, then brush a little egg around the edges. Lightly brush the edges of the larger squares or wrapper with egg and place over the filling. Gently press out any excess air and then use your fingers to seal. Place on a baking sheet lightly dusted with flour. Repeat with the remaining squares or wrappers and filling. Cook the pasta in two batches in a large saucepan of salted boiling water for 3 minutes. Drain, reserving a little of the cooking water.

- For the sage butter, heat the butter in a small skillet until it foams. Add the sage leaves and cook for a minute, then whisk in 3−4 tablespoons of the cooking water to form a sauce. Arrange the pasta on plates and drizzle over the sauce. Serve sprinkled with the amaretti biscuits.

 Easy Sweet Potato and Sage Penne

Cook the sweet potato as above, adding 14 oz penne to the pan and cooking until al dente. Drain and return to the pan, then toss through a handful of chopped sage leaves, 2 tablespoons butter, and ¼ cup grated Parmesan cheese. Serve immediately.

 Sweet Potato and Almond Penne

Cut 2 peeled sweet potatoes into chunks and brush with olive oil. Cook under a preheated medium broiler for 10 −15 minutes or until browned and soft. Meanwhile, cook 14 oz penne according to the package instructions until al dente. Place ⅔ cup almonds and 3 table-spoons water in a food processor or blender and whiz together to form a paste. Heat 2 tablespoons butter in a skillet, add the paste, and cook for 3−5 minutes until thickened. Add ¼ cup grated Parmesan cheese and a squeeze of lemon juice and heat through. Drain the pasta and return to the pan, then stir through the almond sauce and sweet potatoes. Serve immediately.

Index

Page references in *italics* indicate recipes that are illustrated.